NEW MEDIA

in Global Era

Gaurav Yadav

Neha Publishers & Distributors

4832/24, Prahlad Lane, S-207 Ansari Raod, Daryaganj, New Delhi-110002

Published by
Neha Publishers & Distributors
4832/24, Prahlad Lane, S-207 Ansari Raod, Daryaganj,
New Delhi-110002
Tel.: 011-43570976, 23278261
Email-nehapubdistributors@gmail.com

First Edition : 2014

ISBN : 978-93-80318-53-0

Price : 550/-

Laser Typesetting by : JEE-VEE Graphics

Printed at: Vikas Computers, Delhi

PRINTED IN INDIA

Published by Neha Publishers & Distributors, New Delhi-110002

To "Ubee", My Mother

Preface

In the recent years, Change or transformation, is the natural order of the world, even when it is slow and over such a long period of time that it is imperceptible to short-lived and impatient human beings. We, of course, are constantly engaged in a process of change, just by living, but also by the exertion of our will and in particular, the imposition of our inventions, our cultures and our economies on the world.

During the past decade, the growth of digital technology has led to the burgeoning of on-line and mobile communication technologies. There has also been an associated reduction in the cost and size of equipment available to the media while its capacity and capability has also improved. Moves to dismantle the boundaries between traditional areas because of the use of new technologies have begun to transform the new way to produced, received, accessed and interpreted

There are many issues to contemplate and assess in relation to this subject, but here we discuss some but effective contribution to the debate on how new media are transforming and contributing in society.

Author

Contents

Advertising a Big Challenges for Big Companies in Today's Environment

Introduction

I was watching the TV and changing the channels with the remote, and discussing with my wife how the same advertising is modified to various languages and how it is developed. Today it is a main challenge for the multinationals to convenience the people in the various countries and communicate the information about their product and services to the local consumers living there due to the Globalization.

Globalisation has expanded the area of market for business. Earlier, businesses were restricted to domestic market. Today they have grown and market is transformed into multilingual global markets. It is become imperative for the marketer to be sensitive to the cultural differences. Certain products are tradition free global products like technological, scientific or financial products. Selling proposition for such product is performance based. So advertising appeal can be uniform and global. Whereas some products are culture bound and are deeply rooted in national, local or sub-cultural traditions like food, entertainment, travel etc. Advertising for such products demand adaptation as per the local market. Global products allow more content sharing and more media co-ordination whereas culture bound products demand imaginative way of communicating so that product fits in the new tradition. This article aims at analyzing the challenges prevailing in cross cultural advertising. Language barrier and value system of the societies are the most stipulated topic of discussion for cross cultural advertising.

Worldwide, advertising plays an important role. In case of majority of products and markets, it is the successful advertising campaign, which determines the total sales as well as acceptance of the product in the market. There are several important considerations in the design of international advertising and what it communicates. One important consideration is whether to standardize advertising worldwide or to adapt it to match the environment of each country. The important environmental factor which is most important from advertising point of view is culture.

Culture affects everything we do. This applies to all areas of human life from personal relationships to conducting business abroad and advertising. When interacting within our native cultures, culture acts as a framework of understanding. However, when interacting with different cultures this framework no longer applies due to cross cultural differences. In this condition the marketer have to develop a new communicating instrument for its product and services.

Key words: *Cross cultural Advertising, Standardised Advertising, Localised advertising*

Intercultural communication is of importance to international businesses and advertising as it examines how people from different cultures, beliefs and religions come together to work and communicate with each other.

Demands for intercultural communication skills for advertising are increasing as more and more businesses go global or international. Companies realize that there are barriers and limitations when entering a foreign territory. Without the help of intercultural communication they can unknowingly cause confusion and misunderstandings in there advertising. For these intercultural businesses to breach the cultural barriers encountered when stepping into foreign grounds it is vital for them to fully understand the cultural differences that exist so as to prevent damaging business relations due to intercultural communication gaps and misrepresentation of the message in the advertising.

Globalisation, the expansion of intercontinental trade, technological advances and the increase in the number of companies dealing on the international stage have brought about a dramatic change in the frequency, context and means by which people from different cultural backgrounds interact.

Cross cultural solutions to international business advertising demands are increasingly being viewed as a valid and necessary method in enhancing communication and interaction in and between companies, between companies and customers and between colleagues.

Cross cultural consultancies are involved in aiding companies to find solutions to the challenges in cross cultural differences.

The slogan employed by the computer games manufacturer, EA sports "Challenge Everything"raises grumbles of disapproval in religious or hierarchical societies where harmonious relationships are maintained through values of respect and non-confrontation. These differences make the original advertising campaign redundant. It is therefore, critical to any cross culture advertising campaign that an understanding of the particular culture is required. When advertising the cultural values of the society must be analyzed carefully for.

- Is there one religion practiced by majority of the population or multiple religions?
- Is the society individualist or collectivist?
- Is it family oriented? Is it hierarchical?
- Is the society feminist or masculinity?

All these factors should determine the content of the advertising. For instance, advertisement which stresses more on individual gain and achievement will have negative impact on collectivist society. Similarly love and affection between male and female can be showcased in the advertisement targeted for feminist society but which would be ineffective for masculine society. The study of cross cultural advertising is become subject of increasing importance in recent years because of following reasons

- As the integration of world economies has increased significantly in recent years and as nations of the world have international trade has achieved phenomenal growth resulting in increased international advertising across diverse culture.
- Recent changes in world like democratization of Eastern Europe and its transformation into market economy,

reunion of Germany, formation of EU, economic growth of newly industrialized countries and opening of markets in Asia and Latin America have revitalized the global market and encouraged many marketers to expand their business to international market.

- One of the major issues of debate about globalization among the advertisers and researchers is whether or not the consumers around the world are becoming homogenous in terms of taste, preference and values.
- The "cultural imperialism" issue has attracted a great deal of attention over the influence of western advertising and other media product developing nations.

International and national businesses are ultimately the result of people. As with incompatible software, if people are running on different cultural coding, problems can occur. Cross cultural consultancies therefore concentrate their efforts on interpersonal communication.

Different cultures and cultural backgrounds between a highly diverse staff base brings with it obstacles, challenges and difficulties. Cross cultural differences manifest in general areas such as in behaviour, etiquette, norms, values, expressions, group mechanics and non-verbal communication. These cross cultural differences then follow on through to high level areas such as management styles, corporate culture, marketing, advertising, HR and PR.

Role of Cross Cultural Consultant

In order to overcome potential pitfalls, specialist attention is required in the form of a cross cultural consultant for advertising. As one would approach a doctor for a medical diagnosis or an accountant to examine finances, cross cultural consultants offer the expertise, experience and know-how to diagnose problems and provide solutions to interpersonal cultural differences for advertising campaign.

Within companies there are many facets in which cultural differences manifest. Some key areas which cross cultural consultants deal with include, but are not exclusive to, the following:

Cross Cultural HR for Advertising

HR covers a wide range of business critical areas that need cross cultural analysis. Consultants may offer advice on a number of areas including recruitment, relocation, international assignments, staff retention and training programmes.

Cross Cultural Team-Building in Advertising

In order to have a well functioning business unit within a company, communication is critical. Cross cultural consultants will provide tools and methods to promote staff integration, reduce cross cultural conflicts and build team spirit. This is essentially done through highlighting differences and building on strengths to ensure they are used positively.

Cross Cultural Synergy in Advertising

International mergers, acquisitions and joint-ventures require people from different cultural backgrounds to harmonise in order to succeed. Cross cultural consultants counsel on group mechanics, communication styles, norms, values and integration processes.

Cross Cultural Awareness Training for Advertising

Working with colleagues, customers or clients from different cultural backgrounds, with different religions, values and etiquettes can occasionally lead to problems. Cross cultural awareness training is usually a generic introduction into a culture, country, region or religion. The aim is to equip the trainee with the adequate knowledge to deal comfortably with people from different cultures, avoiding misunderstandings and mistakes.

Cross Cultural Training for Expatriate Relocation

Staff that travel overseas need to understand the cultural basics of the host country or region. Knowledge of the country's history, culture, laws, traditions, business practices and social etiquettes all help to minimise the impact of culture shock and hence smooth their transition overseas.

Cross Cultural Negotiations equipped with their knowledge of the two or more cultures that can be meeting around the negotiation table, a cross cultural consultant advises on areas such as negotiation strategies, styles, planning, closure and etiquette in order to increase the chance of a successful outcome, free from misunderstandings, suspicions and general cross cultural communication breakdown.

Cross Cultural PR Consultancy brand image, public relations and advertising are all areas companies must be careful of when moving out of the national context. Tastes and values change dramatically from continent to continent. It is crucial to understand whether the brand name, image or advertising campaign is culturally applicable in the target country. Cross cultural consultants examine words, images, pictures, colours and symbols to ensure they fit well with the target culture.

Cross Cultural Language Training for Cross Cultural Advertising

Language training is an area where little investment is made by companies, but where the business advantages are great. Linguistic knowledge goes a long way in bridging cultural gaps and smoothing lines of communication. Cross cultural consultancies provide language training to business staff, moulding their learning to the business environment in which they work.

Some terms of cross cultural understanding within the business world.

Cross cultural understanding simply refers to the basic ability of people within business to recognise, interpret and correctly react to people, incidences or situations that are open to misunderstanding due to cultural differences. The fundamental intention of cross cultural training is to equip the learner(s) with the appropriate skills to attain cross cultural understanding.

Once the foundations of cross cultural understanding have been laid, the learner(s), either through continued training or experiences within the workplace, gradually attains a more acute appreciation of cultural differences. The different types of appreciation are cross **cultural knowledge**, cross cultural awareness, cross cultural sensitivity and cross cultural competence. Although all the terms may appear similar in meaning, subtle differences exist between them.

'Cross Cultural Knowledge' is critical to basic cross cultural understanding. Without it cross **cultural appreciation** cannot take place. It refers to a surface level familiarization with cultural characteristics, values, beliefs and behaviours.

'Cross Cultural Awareness' develops from cross cultural knowledge as the learner understands and appreciates a culture internally. This may also be accompanied by changes within the learner's behaviour and attitudes such as a greater flexibility and openness.

'Cross Cultural Sensitivity' is a natural by-product of awareness and refers to an ability to read into situations, contexts and behaviours that are culturally rooted and be able to react to them appropriately. An suitable response necessitates that the actor no longer carries his/her own culturally determined interpretations of the situation or behaviour (i.e. good/bad, right/wrong) which can only be nurtured through both cross cultural knowledge and awareness.

'Cross Cultural Competence' is and should be the aim of all those dealing with multicultural clients, customers or colleagues. 'Competence' is the final stage of cross cultural understanding and signifies the actor's ability to work effectively across cultures. Cross cultural competency is beyond knowledge, awareness and sensitivity in that it is the digestion, integration and transformation of all the skills and information acquired through them, applied to create cultural synergy within the workplace.

Cross cultural communication aims to help minimise the negative impact of cross cultural differences through building common frameworks for people of different cultures to interact within. In business, cross cultural solutions are applied in areas such as HR, team building, foreign trade, negotiations and website design(discussed latter in the article).

Effective Cross Cultural Advertising/ Communication

Cross cultural communication solutions are also critical to effective cross cultural advertising. Services and products are usually designed and marketed at a domestic audience. When a product is then marketed at an international audience the same domestic advertising campaign abroad will in most cases be ineffective.

The essence of successful advertising is convincing people that a product is meant for them. By purchasing it, they will receive some benefit, whether it be lifestyle, status, convenience or financial. However, when an advertising campaign is taken abroad to other country, different values and perceptions as to what enhances status or gives convenience exist. These differences make the original advertising campaign defunct.

It is therefore critical to any cross cultural advertising campaign that an understanding of a particular culture is required before presenting advertising to the people.

Language in Cross Cultural Advertising

It may seem somewhat obvious to state that language is key to effective cross cultural advertising. However, the fact that companies persistently fail to check linguistic implications of company or product names and slogans demonstrates that such issues are not being properly addressed.

in India same advertising is used in the various regional parts with the change in the language only and all other elements are same, the advertising convey the same meaning to the target consumers.

The advertising world is littered with examples of linguistic cross cultural blunders. Of the more comical was **Ford's introduction of the 'Pinto' in Brazil**. After seeing sales fail, they soon realised that this was due to the fact that Brazilians did not want to be seen driving a car meaning 'tiny male genitals'.

Language must also be analysed for its cultural suitability. For example, the slogan employed by the computer games manufacturer, EA Sports, "Challenge Everything" raises grumbles of disapproval in religious or hierarchical societies where harmonious relationships are maintained through the values of respect and non-confrontation.

It is imperative therefore that language be examined carefully in any cross cultural advertising campaign.

Communication Style in Cross Cultural Advertising

Understanding the way in which other cultures communicate allows the advertising campaign to speak to the potential customer in a way they understand and appreciate. For example, communication styles can be explicit or implicit. An explicit communicator (e.g. USA) assumes the listener is unaware of background information or related issues to the topic of discussion and therefore provides it themselves. Implicit communicators (e.g. Japan) assume the listener is well informed on the subject and minimises information relayed on the premise that the listener will understand from implication. An explicit communicator would find an implicit communication style vague, whereas an implicit communicator would find an explicit communication style exaggerated.

Colours, Numbers and Images in Cross Cultural Advertising

Even the simplest and most taken for granted aspects of advertising need to be inspected under a cross cultural microscope. Colours, numbers, symbols and images do not all translate well across cultures.

In some cultures there are lucky colours, such as red in China and unlucky colours, such as black in Japan. Some colours have certain significance; green is considered a special colour in Islam and some colours have tribal associations in parts of Africa.

Many hotels in the USA or UK do not have a room 13 or a 13th floor. Similarly, Nippon Airways in Japan do not have the seat numbers 4 or 9. If there are numbers with negative connotations abroad, presenting or packaging products in those numbers when advertising should be avoided.

Images are also culturally sensitive. Whereas it is common to see pictures of women in bikinis on advertising posters on the streets of London, such images would cause outrage in the Middle East and Islamic countries.

Cultural Values in Cross Cultural Advertising

When advertising abroad, the cultural values underpinning the society must be analysed carefully.

- Is there a religion that is practised by the majority of the people?

- Is the society collectivist or individualist?
- Is it family orientated?
- Is it hierarchical?
- Is there a dominant political or economic ideology?

All of these will impact an advertising campaign if left unexamined.

For example, advertising that focuses on individual success, independence and stressing the word "I" would be received negatively in countries where teamwork is considered a positive quality. Rebelliousness or lack of respect for authority should always be avoided in family orientated or hierarchical societies.

We can see that the principles of advertising run through to cross cultural advertising too. That is - know your market, what is attractive to them and what their aspirations are. Cross cultural advertising is simply about using common sense and analysing how the different elements of an advertising campaign are impacted by culture and modifying them to best speak to the target audience.

Few successful businesses are now mono-cultural in their make-up. Even if a business or organization is not dealing internationally the chances are that they employ people from foreign countries. At a higher level globalisation has meant companies are having to look further a field for new revenue streams, products, services, etc. This requires working and dealing with people from different cultures.

The leaders of today's organisations and businesses and advertising need to be adept at managing customers of different cultures. They need to be able to grasp the essence of each culture quickly, because culture is so important in shaping customer or employee behaviour. Leaders must also learn to shape culture (at least that in their own organisations) so that it is positive, and aligned with the direction, the organization is taking.

Some quick tips on how to improve intercultural advertiser's qualities,

- Learn about the cultures of people that you work and interact with. Start from scratch and forget your assumptions and stereotypes. There are many free online resources which can help.
- Get a book about intercultural communication and learn about the subject from an academic level works that will go a long way in unravelling the intricacies of cultural differences.
- Take some formal training from intercultural experts. For very little outlay a day course can go a long way in helping you understand how culture impacts you and your work.
- Try and attend events or occasions where you can submerge yourself in another culture. Use the opportunity to observe how people communicate and interact with one another. If you get the chance to travel abroad do the same when there.
- Start listening and paying more attention when dealing with someone from another culture. You will be surprised how much you pick up by slowing down. Don't jump to conclusions and think actions and behaviours through.

- Temper your own communication style. Pay attention to the rate at which you speak, what non-verbal messages you may be sending, ask for confirmation of understanding, avoid using slang and idioms.
- Learn to tolerate uncertainty. There will be a great deal of unknowns when doing business across cultures. Definitive, concrete answers may not always be given. Focus on what you can determine and try to let go of minor details that are unclear.
- Be patient with others and yourself. Don't give-up. A proper intercultural library of knowledge only comes with time.
- Keep on top of your own development. Continually assess your advancement and make adjustments.
- Ask for help and don't be afraid to apologise for mistakes. People generally are appreciative that you are trying to understand them.

The path to effective intercultural advertising is long but not hard. Essentially it is about opening your mind with which comes greater flexibility and creativity. Once you are able to cope with the cross cultural traditions you can easily achieve a position of good advertiser in the eyes of the MNC.

Determining Advertising Strategy in Cross Cultural Communication

Standardization versus Localization

An important strategic decision for international marketing is whether any advertisement campaign developed at home country can be released to other country only after translating it into local languages. Many marketers have the opinion that any good campaign will be successful in all the markets. Some of them believe cultural differences require the campaign to be tailored to each country.

Standardised Approach

Many marketers and scholars believe that universal advertising can work. Many a times it works well. Some great philosophers supports standardized approach, believing that "the desire to be beautiful is universal". They calls for more extensive use of international advertising campaign which incorporates basic appeal which can be effective in all markets.

Many appeals like

- "mother and child"
- "Freedom from pain"
- "glow of health"
- "know no boundaries"

In an empirical research on this subject, in the sample of 500 fortune firms, Donnelly and Ryans *(Hand book of research: international marketing by Subash Jain Page 295, international advertising standardization/adaptation: theoretical Critique)* discovered that 90% of the firms for at least some degree extend their U.S. advertising approach to non- domestic situations. Unilever, a British – Dutch consumer goods producer has a cross border advertising campaign for the Impulse line of fragrances. Unilever's South African subsidiary developed Impulse as a perfumed deodorant. The parent company decided that the line had Pan- European potential. A cross border campaign was developed based on the simple idea: When a woman wears impulse men can't help but give her flowers. It tapped into a provocative consumer insight. It brought together the impulsiveness of the male- female interaction and created an embodiment of that. Theme remained the same, some alteration was done as per the relationship conducted varies from country to country. For example in Italy the boy plucked the flowers from the garden, while in France he bought the flowers In 1983, Levitt(in the book "*the global market byJohn Quelch and Rohit Deshpande"*) argued in his article " Globalization of Markets "that advertising and marketing can be standardized across the nations of different culture. In Levitt's view globalisation is transforming the world into **homo-cultural market** where all the customers can be addressed and persuaded with common advertising appeals and values irrespective of the different cultures they belong to. If this is true the homogenization of culture would be a boon for marketers. Brand and brand image can be standardized without any difficulty across countries and with little adaptation in local market. The debate about the standardization of marketing programme and process is going on for last 45 years. More than 200 research articles have been published in last 40 years. Three schools of thought about cross cultural advertising have been identified: **standardization, adaptation and compromise**.

- Believers of ***standardization approach*** argue that the International market is converging; standardized advertisement can convey the desired meaning to the consumers of different nations with different culture.
- As per the ***adaptation school of thought***, cultural, linguistic, religious and legal barrier demands for customized advertisement for local market.

- Between these two opposing views, proponents of compromise approach suggest a trade off between too far reaching standardization and some advertisement uniformity.

The proponents of the standardized approach give various reasons to support technological, social and cultural factor. In homogenous market in which all the there viewpoint are present some of the important variables which are common are:

- **Costs savings issue is involved**. Once any advertisement is developed it can be transferred to other countries with minimum additional cost.
- **Realization of economies of scale** is possible only by centralizing worldwide advertising activity to home office.
- Standardization permits **full utilization of advertising expertise** in home office.
- It **prevents the generation of disparate messages** in different nation which eventually may blur the image of the product.
- **Common approach to advertising** ensures proper concern for corporate wide objectives in promoting the product.
- **Similarities in the usage of media** among specific segments across nations justify the standardized approach. For e.g. French and American women belonging to same socio-economic segment have similar media consumption pattern. That means the behavior of consumers of particular segment in one country is

comparable to the consumer of same segment of othet country.

Thus business people in France may exhibit same behavior as of U.S., Egypt or Singapore. Feasibility of standardization depends on related variables like economic, legal, standardized advertising is recommended. But when the variables are heterogeneous across the markets, customized advertisement would be effective. Standardized advertisement is difficult if the use of media and advertisement execution elements are restricted, for example in Malaysia use of foreign models in advertisement is prohibited .Education and income level of the target group has to be kept in mind for advertisement execution .For instance, the advertising message in Sweden tries to inform the target market, purpose of Canadian advertising is to remind whereas in Turkey advertising tries to persuade the audience. The competitive environment and stages of product life cycle further hinder the scope of standardised advertisement. Differing needs, consumption habits, priorities in life, makes the use of common message across the market difficult. Mores (societal norms, customs, virtues or values) and religion acts as filters of advertising messages, transforming factual information into culturally interpreted meaning. Culture and local custom serves as an important factor for ad adaptation. Many studies show the persistent need for ad adaptation. For instance an analysis of U.S. companies operating in Europe showed that advertisement was most resistant towards standardization than product or branding before eighties. However, there are many arguments in the favour of standardization especially because of the globalization in last 20 years. Many developing countries like India and China are accessing the status of advertising intensive countries. Advertisers or agencies have consistently argued for ad standardization and the possibility of global message with local communication. Gillette has organized its advertising plans according to regional and cultural clusters like pan Latin America, pan Middle East, pan Africa and pan Atlantic. According to Gillette this is the result of "Convergence" which is based on the belief that the company can identify the same purchase incentives and needs among consumers in regions or countries that are linked by culture, consumer's habit and development. Furthermore, rapidly changing the company's market for products, communication technologies and usage of internet and satellite television influence global advertising.

Media overlaps demands for more standardized advertisement. Product type may have a positive impact on advertisement standardization. Product satisfying universal needs whose ad messages mostly carry context free information are easy to standardize. Most of the ads for global industries like airlines, banks etc. can be standardized. Thus, Gillette may use the same European- style advertising for Australia, New Zealand and South Africa. In Asia the company may link the less economically developed countries of Malaysia, Thailand, The Philippines and Indonesia. It will market Singapore, Hong Kong and Taiwan together but handle Japan, China and India separately.

The overall objective of Gillette's pan-regional strategy is to sell more than 800 products in around 200 countries. Whereas, standardization for global marketing strategy with multi domestic industries like food, remaining sensitive to regional. The product influence on standardization depends on the interaction between product effect and cultural effect.

Products advertised, ad appeals, benefits and themes displayed reflect a particular cultural context. Product influence becomes a weak covariate if cultural differences are huge. Conversely, when countries of similar culture are compared, product influence may be strong enough to override cultural influence.

Localized Advertising

Cultural differences among countries support the localized advertising approach .The argument for customized advertising is cultural differences which make the standardized ad ineffective. A worldwide leader in toiletries introduced toothpaste in market U.S. with the promise of decay prevention it achieved the leadership position. Seeing the success, the product was introduced in Latin America with the same promise. Though company was well established in that part of world, at the end of one year of large scale advertising and selling effort, the product was withdrawn. It could achieve only 3 % market share instead of the 15 % achieved in U.S.

Understanding the influence of national culture is critical to the effectiveness of international advertising. Much research has been performed to show that consumer behaviour is not only economic but it is influenced by sociology, psychology, anthropology and more than all is culture.

Global advertising is more or less uniform across the markets of many countries with some global prototypes in which some sounds and visual effects are used to overcome the barrier of local language and culture. For example Colgate – Palmolive and Coca – Cola often use such prototypes in their advertisement. Localized advertisement can be global in its essence. Contrary to that multinational messages are modified to cater the demands of local market. For example, Goodyear Tire & Rubber in 39 countries used a slogan "Goodyear, take me home" but there were some differences. In Philippines they stressed certain emotional scenes wherein Brazil they ended the commercial with some joke.

The global product needs global advertising like Benetton, Swatch, and Reebok etc. But in most of the cases adaptation of global messages is required for local market. For instance Levi's Jeans is a global product with globally recognized brand but it targets different market with different advertising appeals.

Sometimes when global advertising mishaps happens, company turns to localized advertising. Initially Parker pen was sold with the support of global advertising across all markets. When in eighties its sale started declining, company adopted different advertising appeal for different as per the demands of local market For market In Germany, printed the achievement of efficient communication and persuasion through advertising messages, it is necessary to change commercials, messages and promotion strategies and to modify them to the demands of local markets and regions. However, modifying the advertisements specifically to the preferences of local market demands creativity. While making the differences in ads, promoters also have to see that possibilities of appearances of unacceptable ads are avoided. In France showing cheese with glass of bear is unaccepted. Commercials showed a hand with

Parker pen writing "This is the way you write with precision." In Great Britain where it was leader old commercials with exotic scenes prevailed. Commercials in U.S.A. stressed on status and image. Consumers of different markets have different motive for purchase and different perception about the image of the product. So even if the company sells same product worldwide, it is not realistic to expect that they will demand uniformed commercials. Standardized advertising approach accordance with the habit of Germans seems particularly unsuited in whereas in France cheese cannot be shown with the glass of wine. Certain modifications in advertisement are done, developing countries where marked differences in lifestyle, level of wealth, market structure, and various other aspects of the environment exist compared with advanced nations. Cultural and economical differences between countries and markets often demand for difference between basic advertising appeal and creative implementation of that appeal to be made on local markets. For instance basic advertising appeal of S. C. Johnson Company for shaving foam "Edge" is smooth saving. To demonstrate this appeal, in U.S.A. company used credit card. A man strokes his face with credit card. The side which used Edge foam is smoother and softer than the other side which used some other brand. Appeal of smooth saving could be spread on to global market. Yet, on many markets, non existence of credit cards would limit creativity of such an appeal so overall efforts would be inefficient.

In manufacturing goods possibilities of using same appeal is more than consumer good. Manufacturing goods are bought and used in the same way and for the same reason in every country. Though there are some possibilities of using same appeal for consumer goods but many researchers believe that consumer goods depend on local demand so it is impossible to use any element of mix marketing on foreign markets. Translating the message is a subject of debate among experts of advertising.

Efficient translation demands:

- Good knowledge of language in which it has to be translated as well as original language,
- Good knowledge of technical aspect of the product and special appeal about the product and ability to write the text which would recreate the affect.

Before deciding whether to make new commercial or translate the same in local language, the expert has to be sure that the text will be accepted and understood by prospective customer. A creative translation is very important than literal one. Well translated message can increase the market share, sale and profit. However, hundreds of examples are there of wrong translation and formulation. For instance, Chevrolet's new car "Nova" was not accepted in Spanish market .The literal meaning of"Nova" in Spanish is star. However when spoken it sounds like "No va" means doesn't go. General Motors changed the name of the car to "Caribe". Marketers who don't understand the local language can do major blunders through improper translation. When Kentucky Fried Chicken (KFC) entered the Chinese market, they discovered that their slogan "Finger lickin' good "came out as "Eat your fingers off." An important assignment of managers in globally oriented business is to understand all the limitations of foreign market like cultural differences, limitations of media, regulation etc. and design the advertising strategy which will enable the real message to be transferred at the right time and in the right manner to the prospective customers. In the process the company can sustain failure if the message does not reach the recipient due to inadequate media and even if message is received and understood it will not affect the market if researcher didn't evaluate the needs and desire of target market adequately. Managers, who understand the process of communication can, more efficiently develop program of global promotion under condition of varied environment.

Though many companies follow the reactions of people to strategy of modifying standardized advertisement based on local market demand but sometimes implementation of such strategy becomes difficult. For instance Different functions of product in different markets. In Europe advertisement commercials and a very successful advertisement in U.S.A. for known brand of perfume "Charlie" which shows behavior of an emancipated woman didn't have any success in South American nations. Bottled mineral water is used for its mineral ingredients while in U.S.A. it is used regardless. Managers of Internationally oriented companies must understand that decisions on standardization or difference in lifestyle modification of advertising. Advertisement of P&G for the shampoo "Wash and go" didn't succeed in Poland because the local culture was not kept in mind. The advertisement showed a woman coming from the pool to take a shower. However, in Poland very small percentage of people has pools while majority have bath not shower. Different stages of product life expectancy. At the time of considerably depend on motivation of o consumers of that particular market. If consumers of different market buy the same product for different reasons then the strategy must respect that difference. On the other hand when consumers from different markets react similarly to certain stimuli it is not necessary to create different advertising messages. As Jacob Hornik explains, "Product universality cannot imply hyperinflation in Federal global message appeal".

Different desires of consumers and Advertising

People in different countries can show different willingness to buy the same product which can influence the conception of global commercials. Also people may have similar visions in life but different wishes because of different views towards accepted ways of realization of their vision.-

Attitudes of Customer

In some countries attitudes of consumers, American women might manifest the same need for cosmetics, but this certainly does not mean that an Israeli woman perceives the American cosmetic ad the same way it is perceived by the American. Therefore, understanding consumer wants, needs, motives and behavior is a necessary condition to the development of an effective promotional program."

Intercultural Communications and Differences

In the last few decades the intercultural communications field has increasingly gained importance within politics, trade and commerce. Both international and national companies are now realizing that a clash of cultures can and does have an adverse affect on business success.

This clash takes place both on an international level, with staff frequently being sent abroad to conduct business and on a domestic level, with an increasingly diverse and multi-cultural UK workforce. The interdependent, global and multi-cultural marketplace of the 21st century brings with it new challenges.

Intercultural awareness seeks to minimise such consequences and maximise the potential of businesses advertising by equipping them with the appropriate tools to communicate across cultures effectively.

Many will ask what intercultural differences impact upon business advertising. By way of highlighting this it may be useful to briefly look at UK business culture and advertising. If a foreigner were to come to work or conduct business and advertising in the UK what areas may they find different?

Let us consider punctuality. Most North American and European countries are 'clock conscious'. Time is money, being late for an appointment is the height of bad etiquette and coming in late to work is unprofessional. However, in many other countries this is not so. Being late for work or an appointment is acceptable and would not have harmful repercussions.

Compared with other countries, the UK office can be a reasonably relaxed and informal environment. Conversations can become personal, humour is seen as a positive and relationships frequently switch between that of friends and colleagues depending on the situation. A new German or Japanese colleague may at first find this unprofessional and lacking in professionalism.

Brainstorming, gaining consensus and objective criticism are all part of the British business meeting. However, in hierarchical cultures none of the above would take place. Meetings are usually the forum for decisions to be conveyed rather than made, criticising or challenging the ideas of colleagues and seniors would be completely unacceptable and would result in the loss of honour and face.

There are numerous illustrations of business culture that a foreigner may need to understand before working with the British. If a person came to the UK and was unaware of such issues they may very well be misunderstood if they were constantly late, never contributed in meetings or did not join in with office banter.

The breadth and scope of cross cultural understanding applies to many fields in the business and personal spheres. Many cross cultural experts focus on the application of cross cultural communication to business and related areas such as negotiation, advertising and marketing. Others promote the idea that cross cultural awareness is necessary in most aspects of 21st century life due to the international nature of the world today. Therefore art, music and TV are also areas where cross cultural awareness becomes relevant.

A recent example of poor cross cultural sensitivity occurred with the launching of a new TV show in the Middle East.

The television show 'Big Brother', where contestants are kept under lock and key inside the same house until public voting leaves a winner, was first launched in the UK on Channel 4 in 2001. It has gone on to see spin off versions in countries such as Russia, Turkey and Australia.

In early 2004, the Arab TV channel MBC surprisingly decided to produce their own version, Al-Ra'is (the Boss), in Bahrain. Perhaps just as unsurprising was the decision to cancel the show after its second showing following intense media criticism accompanied by protests on the streets of Bahrain.

One can only wonder how the MBC producers failed to see the cross cultural implications of Al-Ra'is. An understanding that the format and logistics of the show demanded some cross cultural modifications became manifest as the producers decided to segregate the sleeping quarters of the male and female contestants. In addition a prayer area, women's lounge and mixed-sex communal area were introduced to better accommodate Islamic principles.

Targeting an audience comprising of mainly Muslims, Al-Ra'is failed to read the cross cultural signs. The close quarter interaction between men and women was culturally unacceptable to the majority of viewers. "It is normal for males and females to mix, but not to put them together in the same house for a long time," said 21-year-old student Maryam al-Sayrafi, who summed up most Muslims' feelings on the show.

The failure of Al-Ra'is points to two things:

(1) the adverse consequences of a failure to incorporate cross cultural analysis into a business strategy; in this case a TV show, and

(2) the importance of cross cultural understanding in transferring ideas and concepts across cultures.

Role of PR Department in Maintaining Business and Advertising Campaign

The Public Relations (PR) industry is responsible for creating and maintaining relationships between clients and customers. Through areas such as brand management, advertising, media relations and crisis management, PR practitioners seek to foster interest, trust and belief in a product or company.

PR practitioners are aware of how best to carry this out when dealing within their own nations and cultures, however, when dealing with a foreign audience it is critical that cross cultural differences are recognized and business policy is modified accordingly.

By way of illustrating the impact cross cultural awareness can have on the success or failure of a PR and advertising campaign a brief example can be cited:

Pepsodent tried to sell its toothpaste in Southeast Asia by emphasizing that it "whitens your teeth." They found out that the local natives chew betel nuts to blacken their teeth because they found it attractive. Had the PR company behind this campaign analysed the cross cultural issues related to Pepsodent's product, the failure of this PR campaign could have been avoided.

Cross cultural differences can make or break a PR and advertising campaign. It is therefore crucial that PR practitioners dealing with campaigns that incorporate a cross cultural element analyse likely cross cultural differences. A few key areas shall be highlighted in order to help PR practitioners and advertisers begin to consider how culture may affect future projects.

Language, Culture and Advertising

In order for a PR and advertising campaign to be successful abroad, an appreciation of the target language and its cultural nuances is necessary. The PR and advertising industries are littered with examples of poor translations and a lack of cross cultural understanding leading to PR and advertising failure.

For example, when Ford launched the 'Pinto' in Brazil they were puzzled as to why sales were dead. Fortunately they found out that Brazilians did not want to be seen driving a car meaning 'small male genitals' and promptly changed the name.

Translation of documents, slogans, advertising and literature must be checked and double checked for meanings and cross cultural nuances. This should not only take place between languages but also within languages. Even in English there are cross cultural differences in meanings. For example, the airline UAL headlined an article about Paul Hogan, star of Crocodile Dundee, with, "Paul Hogan Camps it up" which unfortunately in the UK and Australia is slang for "flaunting homosexuality".

The Spoken Word and Advertising

Areas where the spoken word is used in PR and advertising, such as press conferences or interviews, should be prepared for within a cross cultural framework. In short, speaking styles and the content used differs across cultures.

British and American communication styles are described as 'explicit', meaning messages are conveyed solely through words. Correlating background information is deemed necessary and divulged, ambiguity is avoided and spoken words have literal meaning. In many other cultures, communication is 'implicit'. The message listeners are likely to interpret is based on factors such as who is speaking, the context and non-verbal cues. Spoken words do not fully convey the whole story as listeners are expected to read between the lines.

With relation to content, speakers must be aware of the cross cultural differences in humour, metaphors, aphorisms and anecdotes. In addition, references to topics such as politics and/ or religion can be a very sensitive issue in other cultures.

When the spoken word is used the cross cultural distinctions of the target culture must be incorporated in order to help the speaker appeal to and identify with the audience.

The Written Word and Advertising

Press releases, features and copywriting all require a certain amount of cross cultural sensitivity when being applied abroad. Journalistic traditions, writing styles, news worthiness, delivery systems and whether a 'free press' exists are all areas that will affect how the written word is tailored.

In addition, the most important point, from a cross cultural perspective, is how to write in a way that engages the readers in that society or culture. Some cultures may prefer colourful and inspirational writing, others factual and objective. Some may be motivated by language that incorporates a religious or moral tone, others by a money-orientated or materialistic one.

When writing, the first step should always be to look at and integrate the cross cultural particulars of the target audience.

Communication Channels and Advertising

PR practitioners and advertisers employ many different communication channels for advertising trying to circulate information relating to their campaign. The main channels of communication in the UK or America are the radio, the press, TV, internet and public spaces. However, these channels may not always be applicable abroad for advertising.

In many countries the radio, TV or newspapers may not be the primary source of information. Literacy rates may be poor and/or radios may be expensive. In Africa, only 1.4% of the population have access to the internet. Even where such channels of communication do exist, such as TV, some methods used by PR practitioners, namely guerrilla marketing, would be interpreted differently in foreign countries. For example, interrupting live TV may be laughed at in the UK but in other countries it would be seen as irresponsible and rebellious.

The usual channels of communication and advertising in some countries would simply have no effect in terms of PR. In such countries, local alternatives need to be sought such as religious leaders, tribal chiefs, school teachers or NGO's. Information coming from such figures will not only reach the audience but be perceived as more credible than if it were from foreigners.

PR Materials and Advertising

The use of publicity materials in PR campaigns such as logos, slogans, pictures, colours and designs must all be cross culturally examined. Pictures of seemingly innocuous things in one culture could mean something different in another. For example, a company advertised eyeglasses in Thailand by featuring a variety of cute animals wearing glasses. The ad failed as animals are considered to be a low form of life in Thailand and noself respecting .A soft drink was introduced into Arab countries with an attractive label that had a six-pointed star on it. The Arabs interpreted this as pro-Israeli and refused to buy it.

Intercultural awareness is necessary for two reasons. Firstly, it minimises the possibility of misunderstandings and/or the causing of offense through intercultural mishaps. Secondly, it is a means to maximising the potential of business relationships through the utilization of intercultural differences productively.

Some tips for Cross Cultural Communication

One area within the business environment in which intercultural awareness is a necessity is in the business presentation. Directors, managers, salespeople, consultants and business personnel are regularly required to deliver presentations. However, when one is asked to give a presentation to an audience from a different culture there are intercultural factors that can hinder the success of a presentation.

Presentation Language

The language you use in a cross cultural presentation is important. Although the majority of the language that is used in a cross cultural presentation will be understood by an English speaking foreign audience, a speaker must be careful when it comes to slang, idioms or phrases.

If an Englishman were to talk of being "knocked for six" or "bowled over" he may very well be met with puzzled expressions. More subtly, when an American talks of a 'billion' he means a thousand million, whereas in the UK this would mean a million million. Try to keep language simple.

Body Language in Advertising

Pay attention to your body language in a cross cultural presentation. Some cultures are quite animated and will appreciate hand gestures and the expression of emotion through the body. Others expect speakers to remain calm and would find such behaviour over the top. Similarly pay attention to the use of gestures. The thumbs up may mean 'good' in the USA but it means something very different in Iran. Eye contact can also be a major intercultural difference. Some cultures consider strong eye contact a sign of sincerity, others find it overbearing and an invasion of privacy. Do your cross cultural homework before a presentation.

Time of Advertising

Be aware of different approaches to time across cultures. Some cultures prefer a structured, timetabled approach to conducting business affairs, others are more casual. In countries where a start time is considered a guide rather than a definite, allow time for networking or engage in some chit chat until others arrive. Oppositely, if you arrive late to a meeting in a punctual culture, expect some negative feedback. Always show the appropriate stiffness or flexibility depending on the culture.

Emotions in Advertising

Some cross cultural presentations may be in front of a small number of people and deal with sensitive issues in a pressured environment. In such intercultural situations one should always keep their emotions in check. In some cultures a certain amount of cross examination or scrutiny may occur. If this happens bear in mind the positive intentions behind such actions, i.e. the questions are only being posed to establish facts, not to undermine you. Never lose patience, show frustration or display anger. To do so will lead to a loss of credibility.

Style of Presentation

Different cultures learn and take in information in varying ways. One should always try and tailor their presentation style to meet the needs of the target culture. Some cultures, such as Europeans, prefer information to be presented in detail and in a way that sets down foundations that act as the support to a final argument or point. In such a presentation the speaker should gradually lead the audience, using a logical succession of points, to a conclusion. On the other hand, some cultures, like the US, prefer a much faster paced presentation that is bottom-line orientated, meaning the presenter speaks from a point rather towards a point.

Use of Technology in Advertising

Power Point is not the default method of giving a presentation across the world. Some countries many not even have the technical capabilities to accommodate this so one would need to adapt to the resources at hand, whether it be an Over Head Projector or blackboard. Some cultures do not even like a visual element to presentations and find much more worth in words and personality.

Content in Advertising

In a cross cultural presentation, ensure you tailor the content of a presentation to the audience. Different cultures expect different things from a business presentation. Long term orientated cultures may be excited about future projections and figures, but others would rather learn more about the presenter's credentials, accomplishments and experience. A presenter needs to ask whether the target culture will appreciate factual, statistical information presented visually, or a more personal oratory approach.

Audience Participation

Audiences react in different ways across cultures. Some are very engaging and are willing to participate in exercises and Q&A sessions, others are the opposite. Audiences also show respect in many ways. A Japanese audience may close their eyes while listening; a US one may clap when a good point is made and a Saudi one may do nothing at all.

Although the number of areas where one could point to intercultural differences in presentations is vast, for the sake of brevity the above mentioned areas have been highlighted as a way of drawing attention to some of the major ones. It is hoped these can then act as a foundation to improving ones insight into the way intercultural differences manifest in the business environment.

Global Advertising through Websites and Cross Cultural Issues

With the rise in ownership of computers and internet usage growing daily, the internet is fast becoming the primary port of call for information, shopping and services. In addition, those computer and internet users are increasingly from non-English speaking countries. At the end of 2008, it was estimated that 50% of internet users were non-native English speakers (source.com). This figure is constantly rising. In response, businesses have quickly become aware of the benefits of website localization.

Website localization is the process of modifying an existing website to make it accessible, usable and culturally suitable to a target audience. Website localization is a multi-layered process needing both programming expertise and linguistic and cultural knowledge. If either is missing, the chances are that a localization project will encounter problems.

In the majority of cases it is the lack of linguistic and cultural input that lets a website localization project down. In order to give an insight into the impact culture has on website localization depict in which areas a solid understanding of the target culture is necessary.

Language in Website Localization English to other Languages

Translating a website from English into another language is not as simple as it may appear. There are numerous factors that have to be taken into consideration when translating a websites' content.

Do all the words, phrases, sayings and metaphors translate directly to the target language? Would it be wise to translate the phrase "everyman for himself" in text describing a company or product if this is going to be read by a highly collectivist culture? Does the content of your website use humour and if so will the target culture appreciate or even understand it? Native alternatives should always be sought and used in any website localization.

When translating into another language carefully consider the variants. If it is to be an Arabic website then is aimed at Tunisians or Iraqis, Egyptians or Yemenis? If you are targeting all Arabic speakers then ensure Modern Standard Arabic has been employed by your translator.

One must analyse the style of the language and the target audience. If the audience is foreign business personnel, the vocabulary, grammar and punctuation must reflect this. If the audience is informal or youth orientated then a more relaxed language must used. Just as we in the UK would identify the difference between a site using "posh English" and "street English", other cultures will have the same perceptions of language. Using the wrong language for the wrong reader in your localization project will lead to a misunderstanding of the site or company.

It is essential to assess what information is necessary to carry over into the new site. Do not assume that all information on the English site is automatically transferred over. One must evaluate the target culture and society. Is it a culture that relies on information rich writing to fully understand a concept or product or is a culture that relies more on images or one that needs little text to grasp ideas and concepts? If your English site employs a lot of technical language then consider how best to transfer these concepts without the use of language differences.

Pictures in Website Localization

Images carry many subtle cultural messages within them. These can speak volumes about your company or product. Pictures or images may have certain negative connotations that may repel viewers. This is now an area that thankfully is receiving attention in website localization.

For example, if a travel site in a Muslim populated country used pictures of scantily clad women in bikinis, disco dancing and beer drinking, the chances are that they would not be very successful.

When including pictures of personnel it is wise to tailor these to what the target audience will look positively upon. A picture of the Director behind a desk in an office will be fine for a seniority respecting society, but for an egalitarian society it is better to show the Director mixing with staff.

It is through pictures that websites can either relate to an audience or repel them.

Symbols in Website Localization

As with pictures, symbols can cause problems in localization. Icons using fingers such as an OK sign or V-sign may mean different things to different cultures. Our Western symbols do not always mean the same abroad. An oft(faith) cited example is the representation of the house referring to a home page, or a letterbox to mail. The use of animals in logos can cause embarrassment and further problems. For example, pigs are considered unclean in the Middle East and cows as holy in India.

Colours in Website Localization

Colours are also loaded with cultural meanings that need to be analysed in website localization. Choosing the wrong colour for your logo or background will not always have disastrous consequences, but avoiding them is always advisable.

For example, in Japan white is commonly associated with mourning. In China red is auspicious. In Africa certain colours represent different tribes.

Navigation in Website Localization

It is even the most taken for granted aspects of website layout that must be analysed properly for a successful localization project. In the West we assume that how we present websites is how it naturally should be done. This is far from the truth.

A common problem experienced in localization is the effect on layout through translation. Foreign scripts can make your pages need more room or less room depending on the target language in the localization. Not all languages read from left to right. Arabic is from right to left and both Japanese and Chinese are from top to bottom.

Access to certain pages is also a factor that can be considered as relevant. Highly hierarchical cultures may view a site positively if it is "member only" access, whereas an egalitarian culture may find it disagreeable.

Content in Website Localization

Examining your written content in any localization process in critical to its success. This is not only important for proper transfer of aspects such as dates, currencies, and units of measurement but for the presenting the correct image.

For example, will the site focus on a product or a company? Both bring with them certain considerations dependent on the target culture. If a company is marketing itself in a culture that respects seniority and hierarchy, readers will want to see information on senior members. Along with their titles and rank they will also want to evaluate them through information on their professional qualifications, experience and contacts. These areas in the UK may generally be avoided as in some culture it is bordering on self-indulgence and boasting.

Some Failures of Cross Cultural Advertising

It is crucial for today's business personnel to understand the impact of cross cultural differences on business, trade and internal company organisation. The success or failure of a company, venture, merger or acquisition is essentially in the hands of people. If these people are not cross culturally aware then misunderstandings, offence and a break down in communication can occur.

The need for greater cross cultural awareness is heightened in our global economies and advertising. Cross cultural differences in matters such as language, etiquette, non-verbal communication, norms and values can, do and will lead to cross cultural blunders.

To illustrate this there are a few examples of cross cultural blunders that could have been avoided with appropriate cross cultural awareness training:

Brands which operate on a global scale.

Brand names such as Nike, Coca-Cola, McDonald's, Gillette, Adidas, Disney, Marlboro, Sony, Budweiser, Microsoft and Pepsi are now recognized across the world. The dismantling of trade barriers, combined with the rise of global communications technologies such as the Internet, has meant that companies can expand into new markets faster than ever before.

However, many companies have confused the in era of globalization with an era of homogenization. If they have had success with one product in one market they have assumed they can have equal success in another. All they believe they have to do is set up a Web site in the relevant language, run an ad campaign and set up a similar distribution network. What they forget to understand is that there is more to a country than its language, currency or gross domestic product. The cultural differences between, and often within, countries can greatly affect the chances of success for a brand and advertising campaign.

In order to succeed, brands must cater for the specific tastes of each market they enter. If these tastes change, then the brand must change also. As the bumpy ride experienced by Kellogg's in India indicates, companies which fail to accommodate and acknowledge these vast cultural differences face a long battle in replicating their success at home in other markets. However, understanding cultural differences is not just about international markets. It is also about understanding the specific culture of the brand. When companies acquire a brand that wasn't theirs to begin with, they can often make similar faux pas as when they move into a foreign market. However, instead of making the mistake of misinterpreting the market they misinterpret the brand. This happened when CBS acquired the guitar company Fender and when Quaker Oats bought the soft drink Snapple. Although the companies spent millions on marketing, they lost market share as they didn't understand exactly where the market was, and what the customer wanted. As a result, in both cases, the acquisition weakened the brand.

- **Mercedes-Benz**. In 1995 the German car giant opened a plant in India to produce its E-class Sedan. The car, which was targeted at the growing ranks of India's wealthy middle class, failed to inspire. By 1997, the plant was using only 10 per cent of its 20,000 car capacity. 'Indians turned up their noses at the Sedan – a model older than those sold in Europe,' reported Business Week at the time. 'Now Mercedes has to reassess its mistakes and start exporting excess cars to Africa and elsewhere.'

- **Lufthansa**. Germany's Lufthansa airline joined forces with Indian company, the Modi Group, to launch a new domestic private airline, Modi-Luft, in 1993. However, three years later ModiLuft had gone bust and Lufthansa filed a lawsuit against one of the Modi brothers, claiming he had used funds obtained from the German company in other ventures. In return, the Modi Group accused Lufthansa of charging too much and of producing defective planes.
- **Coca-Cola.** The Coca-Cola company understood that distribution was the key to building a strong Indian brand. It therefore decided to buy out one of India's most successful soft drink companies and manufacturers of popular soda brand Thums Up. However, although this gave Coca-Cola an instant distribution network, Thums Up remained more popular than Coke for many years. Most Indians initially thought that the new entry to the market wasn't fizzy enough.
- **Whirlpool**. When Whirlpool launched its refrigerators on the Indian market, it found the market unwilling to buy larger sizes than the standard 165 litres.

- MTV. When MTV India was launched, the aim was to bring Western rock, rap and pop to the sub-continent. Now, however, the music policy has shifted to accommodate Indian genres such as bhangra.
- **Domino's Pizza**. Initially, Domino's Pizza transferred its Western offerings direct to the Indian market, but the company eventually realized that it had to bow to local tastes, as Arvind Nair, chief executive officer at Domino's Pizza India explains. 'Initially, our focus was to stay only in metropolitan areas, but in the last two years we have felt the need to spread ourselves into "mini metros" and B-category towns. We have also experimented with our taste options, especially when we went into smaller towns. We have focused on more regional flavours now,' he says. As a result of this change of strategy, Domino's came up with localized toppings such as 'Peppy Paneer' and 'Chicken Chettinad'. This move was greeted with a wry smile from Domino's main Indian competitor, US Pizza, which was the first to offer local topping. 'In 1995, when we offered tandoori chicken and paneer toppings, some made fun of us saying, why not offer spaghetti and pasta toppings? The same companies are now offering chole and spicy masala pizzas,' says Wahid Berenjian, the managing director for US Pizza. He told the Hindu newspaper Business Line that US brands such as Domino's made the mistake of thinking that US tastes are universal. 'You cannot change the taste buds that were developed more than a thousand years ago,' he said.

- **Citibank.** When Citibank entered the Indian market, the firm's aim was to target only high-income earners. But, in the words of the Business Line newspaper, Citibank soon realized that 'in India it makes sense to go the mass banking way rather than the class banking way.'
- An American oil rig **supervisor in Indonesia** shouted at an employee to take a boat to shore. Since it is no-one berates an Indonesian in public, a mob of outraged workers chased the supervisor with axes.
- **Pepsodent** tried to sell its toothpaste in Southeast Asia by emphasizing that it "whitens your teeth." They found out that the local natives chew betel nuts to blacken their teeth which they find attractive.
- A company advertised **eyeglasses in Thailand** by featuring a variety of cute animals wearing glasses. The ad was a poor choice since animals are considered to be a form of low life and no self respecting Thai would wear anything worn by animals.
- The **soft drink Fresca** was being promoted by a saleswoman in Mexico. She was surprised that her sales pitch was greeted with laughter, and later embarrassed when she learned that fresca is slang for "lesbian."
- When President George Bush went to Japan with Lee Iacocca and other American business magnates, and directly made explicit and direct demands on Japanese leaders, they violated Japanese etiquette. To the Japanese (who use high context language) it is considered rude and a sign of ignorance or desperation to lower oneself

to make direct demands. Some analysts believe it severely damaged the negotiations and confirmed to the Japanese that Americans are barbarians.

- A soft **drink was introduced into Arab countries** with an attractive label that had **stars on it—six-pointed stars.** The Arabs interpreted this as pro-Israeli and refused to buy it. Another label was printed in ten languages, one of which was Hebrew—again the Arabs did not buy it.
- U.S. and British negotiators found themselves at a standstill when the American company proposed that they "table" particular key points. In the U.S. "Tabling a motion" means to not discuss it, while the same phrase in Great Britain means to "bring it to the table for discussion."
- In addition to interpersonal cross cultural gaffes, the translation of documents, brochures, advertisements and signs also offers us some comical cross cultural blunders like Indian gods.
- **Kellogg** had to rename its Bran Buds cereal in Sweden when it discovered that the name roughly translated to "burned farmer."
- When **Pepsico advertised** Pepsi in Taiwan with the ad "Come Alive With Pepsi" they had no idea that it would be translated into Chinese as "Pepsi brings your ancestors back from the dead."
- American medical containers were distributed in Great Britain and caused quite a stir. The instructions to **"Take**

off top and push in bottom," innocuous to Americans, had very strong sexual connotations to the British.

- In Italy, a campaign for Schweppes Tonic Water translated the name into **"Schweppes Toilet Water."**
- **In a Belgrade hotel elevator.** To move the cabin, push the button for wishing floor. If the cabin should enter more persons, each one should press a number of wishing floor. Driving is then going alphabetically by national order.
- **In a Yugoslavian hotel.** The flattening of underwear with pleasure is the job of the chambermaid.
- **In a Bangkok dry cleaner's.** Drop your trousers here for best results.
- **In an East African newspaper.** A new swimming pool is rapidly taking shape since the contractors have thrown in the bulk of their workers.
- **Detour sign in Kyushi, Japan.** Stop—Drive sideways.
- **At a Budapest zoo.** Please do not feed the animals. If you have any suitable food, give it to the guard on duty.

Mastering Advertising Strategies for Cross Cultural Population

Working across cultures requires a diverse skill set and a different approach from business in general. When bridging cultures both similar and foreign to your own, certain strategies are crucial to international business advertising success. Here are ten strategies for interacting with people from different cultures.

Learn about the business beforehand

The general business strategy becomes increasingly important when dealing with businesses across cultures. Get on their website, check out their promotional material. Get a feel for the atmosphere, attitude, and angle that the business has. Many cultural factors are passed down from the societal level to businesses. However, each organization will have its own culture, personality, and way of doing things.

Observe

Because your mind is processing a lot of information in new environments, your observation skills when working across cultures may be flooded or unfocused. Keep your observation skills engaged and alert to elements that will help you do business. Notice how people act, dress, and treat each other. Especially if you come from a culture that emphasizes verbal communication, make a point of looking for messages that are conveyed without being said. Being able to read a situation will greatly improve your ability to have a successful meeting.

Ask questions

Many people don't want to reveal how little they know about other cultures, so they don't ask questions. Ultimately, they limit their ability to work in other cultures. Questions show you are interested in your colleague's culture. This interest and consideration helps build your relationship, which is especially important if your culture has a reputation for trying to culturally dominate others (e.g. the U.S.). Demonstrate that you are working to create synergy between your cultures with questions.

In doing so, you create room for the mistakes you may make; people are more willing to look past cultural blunders if they know you are trying to learn about the culture you are working with.

Stay aware of yourself

Some people feel like they have somewhat of an out-of-body experience when in cross-cultural situations because they are focused on everything new outside of themselves. There can be so much going on around you that you forget to focus on yourself as well. Take advantage of down time (and make time for it) so you can get in touch with your body and feelings. What's your gut feeling? Where is it coming from? This process can help you feel more grounded and secure in your experience abroad.

Allow for more time

Working across cultures takes more time. Communication may be slowed and logistics may be different. You may be working with a culture with a different concept of time altogether. Expect most things to take longer than they would when dealing with a business from your same culture or country. Also give yourself more time to process all the information before making decisions.

Look for individual differences

Overviews of cultures are meant to be guidelines only. Individuals may have values and behaviors that vary greatly from those of their native culture. Many people make the mistake of trying to fit people they are working with into cultural molds, when often they don't fit. People's values and behaviors are influenced in part by their culture, but also by their background, experiences, and personality. Be careful not to attribute too much of what you observe to a cultural difference.

Find the humor

Humor heals and helps you through difficult situations. Travel can be stressful, as can new environments and change in general. This stress can limit both your flexibility and your ability to handle cross-cultural situations. Combat stress with humor. Be able to step away (at least mentally) from situations and find the humor in them.

Learn to tolerate uncertainty

This is an essential skill, and one that can be extremely difficult for people from some cultures where directness and exactness are valued (e.g. Germany, the US). There will be a great deal of unknowns when doing business across cultures. Definitive, concrete answers may not always be given, especially if you are working with a culture with a high tolerance for uncertainty. Focus on what you can determine and try to let go of minor details that are unclear. (Similarly, if you come from a culture that doesn't place a high value on exactness and are working with someone from a culture that does, try to provide clarification and details when possible.)

Go early

If your meeting is face-to-face and you'll be traveling abroad, go a few days before your scheduled meeting. Give yourself time to adjust; you will have to deal with physical adjustments (jet lag, different foods) as well as a number of cultural adjustments as well. These changes can be overwhelming and should be spread out to make them manageable. Give yourself time to adjust physically and then your mind will be better able to make cultural adjustments that are essential for success.

Build your intercultural skills

When working with people from different cultures, you need a solid understanding of the norms of that culture. You also need communication skills and business strategies that can be applied across cultures. The items listed above reflect some of the necessary skills for intercultural work in general. However, individuals need to further their intercultural competence based on their own situations and needs.

Make culture difference new ways to Grasp new Business not barriers

1. **Break Assumptions**

   Everyone makes or has assumptions about others. Assumptions are beliefs rather than objective truth and are usually influenced by a number of subjective factors. For intercultural communication to truly work, people need to assess their assumptions and ask themselves why they hold those ideas or beliefs. By doing so and even openly examining them with others, the initial barrier to intercultural communication is overcome.

2. **Empathise**

   In order to come to appreciate and understand people from different cultures, empathy is vital. Through putting yourself in someone else's shoes you come to see or appreciate their point of view.

3. **Involve**

Involving others in tasks or decision making empowers and builds strong relationships. Using intercultural diversity is in essence a more creative approach to problem solving as it incorporates different points of view.

4. **Discourage Herd Mentality**

Herd mentality refers to a closed and one dimensional approach. Such a ways of thinking curbs creativity, innovation and advancement as people are restricted in how to think approach and engage with people or challenges. Intercultural communication can only flourish and therefore contribute if people are encouraged to think as individuals, bring their cultural influences to the table and share ideas that may be outside the box.

5. **Shun Insensitive Behaviour**

People can and do behave in culturally insensitive ways. By attacking someone's person, you attack their culture and therefore their dignity. This can only be divisive. Intercultural communication is based upon people thinking through words and actions to ensure they do not act inappropriately. When insensitive behaviour is witnessed it is the responsibility of all to shun it and ensure it remains unacceptable.

6. Be Wise

Wisdom is not called wisdom for nothing. People need to be aware how to interact with people with respect and knowledge. Intercultural communication is essentially founded upon wisdom, i.e. showing maturity of thought and action in dealing with people. Through thinking things out and have background knowledge to intercultural differences much of the communication problems witnessed within business could be avoided.

Summary/Sum up

Culture is not constant; it evolves over time. Changes in the value systems can be slow and painful for the society. Changes, however, does occur and can often be quite profound. The culture of the societies also changes as they become richer, because economic progress affects a number of other factors, which in turn impact on culture. Increased urbanization and improvements in the quality and availability of education are both a function of economic progress and both can lead to declining emphasis on the traditional values associated with poor rural societies.

Globalisation is an inevitable process in 21st century so is the cross-culturisation.

In 21st century from a marketing point of view it is very important for marketers to realize that as the world is becoming more homogenous and becomes globalized, cultural distinctions between national market are not only fading but for some product it will disappear altogether. To be aware of and sensitive to the cultural differences is a major premise for the Global corporations such as Hitachi, Disney, Microsoft, Levi Strauss etc. whose products and operations are success in the 21st marketplace. In this dynamic world around the globe, are creating the conditions for the **Not only does culture influence marketing, but marketing also merging of cultures.** With such influences culture Marketers can make McDonald's hamburgers in China, Levi's in India, Sony Walkmans in South Africa and MTV everywhere helping to foster an ubiquitous youth culture and conditions for less cultural variations. However, on the other hand, differences among nations, regions and ethnic groups in terms of cultural factors are far from distinguishing but become more obvious. There are counter trends such as religious fundamentalism in many countries, the separatist movement

In an increasingly modern and materialistic world, some societies are trying to re-emphasize their cultural roots and uniqueness. Thus, just because people over the world were blue jeans and eat at McDonald's, one should not assume that they have adopted American values. Many states are claiming for a right to culture in recent years that might initiate a worldwide cultural protectionism for trans-national marketing and advertising while we are approaching the globalization economically in as agents of changes within the culture .The interaction between marketing advertising and culture can be examined from three perspectives.

First, culture defines acceptable purchasing and product-use bhaviour for both consumers and business. In the culture where business gifts are expected but not presented would be an insult to the host. In the culture where gifts generate obligation like Japan, it may be beneficial to engage in the practice. Yet, in the other cultures, offering the business gifts could be misinterpreted.

Secondly each element of culture influences each element of marketing mix. Advertising is very much influenced by language and communication style. Product acceptance is affected by culturally based attitudes towards change.

Thirdly, marketing also influences culture, especially by contributing to cultural borrowing and change. As more markets become global, the rate of cultural changes will also increase. Marketing cross-culturally is a process during which marketers need to constantly adjust their behaviours and marketing programs to suit the target markets. However, when entering foreign markets, marketers frequently fall into the trap of the self reference criterion, the unconscious application of one's own cultural experiences to a market in another culture. Marketers also tend to suffer from ethnocentrism, belief that one' own culture is superior to any other culture. It is important for the marketers to know that there is no room for ethnocentrism in 21st century marketing place.

References

1. Advertising Phoenix Publication house Pvt. Ltd., New Delhi (Jethwaney Jaishri)
2. The complete Guide to Advertising MacMillan London, Douglas Torin
3. Advertising: Mass Communication in Marketing Vakils, Feffer & Simons Pvt. Ltd., Bombay little field James.

"Celebrity Advertising in Indian Culture" – Emerging Trends & Challenges under Globalization

INTRODUCTION

In the beginning of the 21st century boundaries across nations have been broken and ***Globalization*** *has made the world almost a single homogenous market place, but one cannot ignore the economic, technological and* ***cultural*** *difference that still exist among nations.*

From the snow covered Himalayas in the north to the backwaters of Kerala in the south and from the Bay of Bengal in the east to Mumbai in the west, talk's immensely about the diversity one can expect in India not only in terms of landscape but culture also.

The opening up of the Indian economy in the early 90's paved the way for ***multi national*** *companies to tap the vast Indian market with their product and service offerings. India offers a unique* ***cultural package*** *in terms of religion, languages, life* *style and value system etc. and developing advertising strategy to connect with such diverse* ***target audience*** *is really a challenging proposition.*

With this backdrop in mind the ***objectives*** *of this research paper is to* ***first*** *highlight the* ***emerging trends*** *noticed in marketing communication and celebrity advertising in India.* ***Secondly*** *identifying the* ***challenges*** *encountered by advertisers in regard to celebrity advertising.* ***Finally*** *providing* ***strategic input*** *to advertisers in selecting the right celebrity to connect their brand with their target audience of diverse cultural background under present Global scenario.*

The findings that emerged from the empirical study conducted in Kolkata will be highly beneficial to advertisers and their advertising agencies to successfully communicate their message to the target audience by using celebrities in their advertising campaign.

Introduction

Diversity in every respect, be it in terms of **landscape**, the mountains in the north, the back waters of Kerala in the south or the desert in the west to the Bay of Bengal in the east or in terms of **culture** prevailing in these areas, **food habits** and **dress sense** of the people makes our motherland **India** unique and we can boast of **'unity among diversity'.**

While developing a marketing communication strategy to connect with their target audience advertisers should take in to consideration the cultural aspect of the target audience.

Key words: *Globalization, Celebrity Advertising, Culture, Media & Target Audience.*

Appreciating and understanding the **cultural differences** prevailing in India will be the magic key to success for MNC's trying to explore the vast Indian market

Globalization – Consequence in India.

Globalization has spread its arms far and wide, and developing economies like **India** is also touched by it and experiencing its impact. The last decade of the 20th century opened the flood gates for multinational companies to explore the vast Indian market with their product and service offerings. The domestic players got to face a stiff competition from their counterparts from abroad. Under such competitive and dynamic market situation "**survival for the fittest became the new mantra**".

Companies are finding it really tough to achieve their marketing objective. The 4P's of marketing namely Product, Price, Place and Promotion are to be blended in the right proportion to do justice to their marketing attempt.

Globalization has made the world more nearly a single, homogeneous, market place, but there will always be economic, geographic, cultural and technological difference. Standardization and localization are the two **Marketing Communication** strategies used in International Marketing Communication.

Companies are concentrating on international markets for a number of reasons. Many companies in the **United States and Western Europe** have recognized that their domestic markets offer them limited opportunities for expansion because of slow population growth, saturated markets, intense competition and /or unfavourable marketing environment.

International Environment

Companies engaging in international marketing must carefully analyze the major environmental factors of each market in which they compete, including economic, demographic, cultural and political/legal variables. These factors are important in evaluating the potential of each country as well as designing and implementing a marketing and promotional strategy.

Forces in International Marketing Environment

Companies stepping out of their comfort zone from their place of origin to explore the opportunities in other countries must take note of the following factors while developing their marketing and promotional strategy.

Economic Environment	Cultural Environment
• Stages of Economic Development	• Language
• Economic Infrastructure	• Life style
• Standard of Living	• Values
• Per capita Income	• Norms and Customs
• Distribution of wealth	• Ethics and Moral standards
• Exchange rates	• Taboos
Demographic Environment	**Political/Legal Environment**
• Size of Population	• Government Policies
• Number of Households	• Laws and regulations
• Age Distribution	• Political Stability
• Occupation Distribution	• Nationalism
• Education Levels	• Attitude towards MNC's
• Employment Rate	
• Income Levels	

Understanding Cultural Environment

Cultural variables marketers must consider include language, custom, tastes, attitudes, lifestyles, values and ethical/moral standards. Almost every nation exhibits **cultural traits** that influence not just needs and wants of consumers but how they go about satisfying them.

Marketers must be sensitive not only in determining what products and services they can sell in foreign cultures but also in communicating with them. Advertising is often the most effective way to communicate with potential buyers and create markets in other countries.

Advertisers can encounter problems with the connotative meaning of sign and symbols used in their messages. **Pepsodent** tooth paste was unsuccessful in **South East Asia** because in its advertising campaign it promised "**White Teeth**" to a culture where black and yellow teeth are symbol of prestige.

Another dimension of culture that is very important for international marketers to understand is **'Values'.** Cultural values are beliefs and goals shared by members of a society regarding ideal end states of life and modes of conduct.

Cultural values in the **United States** place a major emphasis on individual activity and initiative, while many **Asian countries** stress cooperation and conformity to the group. **Indian value system** gives importance to family bonding, togetherness and respect for elders. This is to be reflected in the advertising campaign to successfully connect with the culture of the target audience.

Japan is one of the more difficult markets for many American marketers to understand because of its unique values and customs. The Japanese have a very strong commitment to the group, social interdependence and collectivism are as important to them as individualism is to most Americans. Advertising stressing individuality and nonconformity have traditionally not done well in Japan. Of late westernized values have become more prevalent in Japanese advertising in recent years.

As advertisers turn their attention to **China,** more consideration is also being given to understanding the cultural system and values of the world's most populous country. Chinese values are centered on Confucianism that stresses loyalty and interpersonal relationships.

India is a unique country in terms of the **cultural diversity** exhibited and it becomes very challenging for advertisers and their advertising agencies to establish their brand in the market and connect with their target audience. Many MNC's and domestic players in India are now looking to hire famous **celebrities (especially Hindi Film Stars)** to endorse their brands in order to connect with their target audience.

Emerging Trends in Marketing Communication

In today's dynamic and intense competitive market situation survival for the fittest is the new mantra. There has been a shift from the traditional concept of "**seller's market**" to the new and emerging concept of "**Buyer's market**". The customer is the king in today's context and in India both the MNC's and the domestic players are leaving no stone unturned to connect with their target audience.

The concept of **Integrated Marketing Communication** (IMC) has added a new dimension in the way companies are trying to connect with their target audience. With brands becoming "**me- too**" in terms of features, quality etc. it became all the more challenging for companies to connect with target audience. The traditional promotional mix concept is to be replaced by the new and emerging **Integrated Marketing Communication** concept.

Every brand is trying to create its own identity in the market and advertisers and their advertising agencies are trying to figure out and highlight the **Unique Selling Proposition (USP)** of the brand to their target audience in order to create their own identity and thereby gain competitive advantage.

Brands are relying on different **advertising appeals** be it rational or emotional in their advertising campaign to connect with their target audience. The advertiser's are highlighting **patriotism appeal, fun appeal, health appeal and fear appeal** etc. to persuade their target audience to try out their brand or stay with it.

Role of Advertising Media

In order to reach the target audience with their advertising message to inform and persuade them, companies are relying on the different mass media as their medium of communication. The world of media comprising of **Print media, Electronic media, and Outdoor media as well as new and emerging media like the internet and the mobile** is assuming greater importance in the business of advertising and helping advertiser and their advertising agency to successfully communicate their message to their target audience.

In any advertising campaign a **combination of media** is selected by the advertiser and their advertising agency for two basic reasons. **First,** no one media is good enough to penetrate the entire target market and **secondly** features of one medium cannot be replicated by another.

This media boom and development in communication have made the task of advertiser's really challenging and globalization has added a new dimension to it.

Emerging Trends in Celebrity Advertising

Celebrities are people who are successful in their own profession, who enjoy public recognition and have huge fan following and media attention. Celebrities have the following type of association with the customers of a brand:

(i) **Psycho graphic Connect:** Stars are loved and adored by their fans and advertisers use stars to capitalize on these feelings to sway the fans towards their brand.

(ii) **Demographic Connect:** Different stars appeal differently to various demographic segments (age, gender, income group, occupation etc.).

(iii) **Mass Appeal:** Some stars have a universal appeal to generate interest among the masses.

Celebrity Advertising – Historical Relevance in India

Celebrity advertising in India started gaining prominence since 1980's. The introduction of television added a variable effective medium of communication. Celebrities are people who are recognized by a large group of people. Celebrities may convey a broad range of meanings, involving demographic, personality and lifestyle types.

One of the primary goals of advertising is the persuasion of customers, i.e., the active attempt to change or modify consumer's attitude towards brands. In this respect, the credibility of an advertisement plays an important role in convincing the target audience of the attractiveness of the company's brand.

Pursuing a celebrity endorsement strategy enables advertisers to project a credible image in terms of expertise, persuasiveness, trustworthiness, and objectiveness. Marketers have been leveraging celebrity appeal for a long time.

One can still remember brands like Vimal, Thums-Up, Gwalior and Dinesh using star-appeal in the early days of mass advertising. There was a burst of advertising, featuring stars like Tabassum (Prestige Pressure-cooker), Jalal Agha (Pan Parag Pan-masaala) etc.

Present Scenario in India

The dawn of the 21st century saw the phenomenon of celebrity endorsement gaining increasing prominence in our country. Multinationals as well as domestic companies are going the extra yard to sign up leading Hindi Film stars for endorsing their brands.

In recent times, we had the **Shah Rukh-Santro** campaign with the objective of overcoming the hindrance that an unknown Korean company (**Hyundai Motors**) faced in the Indian market. The objective was to earn faster brand recognition, association and emotional unity with the target group.

A study by **AdEx India**, a division of TAM Media Research, finds that there has been 49 per cent growth in celebrity endorsement ad volumes on TV during 2007 compared to 2006.

Film celebrities accounted for 81 per cent share of overall celebrity endorsement on TV during 2007, with male actors accounting for 50 per cent share and female actors 31 per cent. Sports and TV personalities followed the film celebrities in the endorsements race with 14 and 5 per cent share respectively. The table (Table 1) clearly shows the top Indian celebrities with maximum number of endorsements in 2007 as per a study conducted by AdEx India (A division of TAM Media research).

Table 1

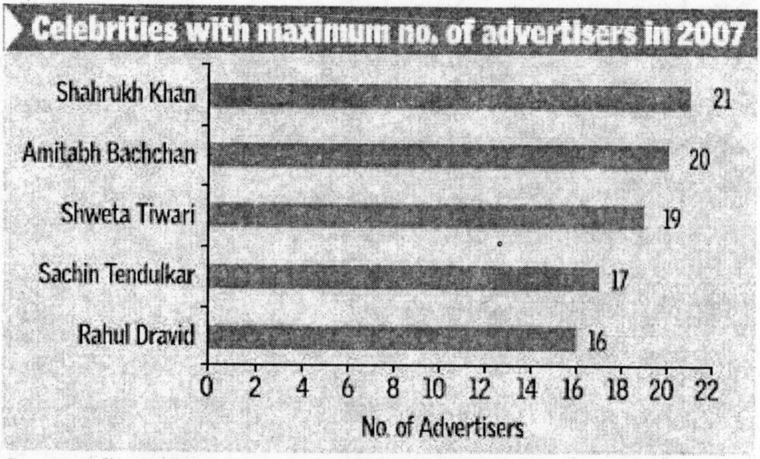

Source: AdEx India (A Division of TAM Media Research)
Note: Figures are based on count of advertisers

The following trends are evident in celebrity advertising :

- **Overshadowing the product-**The target audience may focus their attention on the celebrity and may fail to notice the brand. Company should select a celebrity who can attract attention and convince the target audience, yet not overshadow the brand.
- **Overexposure.** In the beginning of the 21st century it is common to see celebrities endorsing more than one

brand. **Multiple brand endorsement** is common among Indian celebrities and this often brings to light the concept of celebrity **over exposure.**

- **Celebrity branding** is a type of branding, or advertising, in which a celebrity uses his or her status in society to promote a product, service or charity. Celebrity branding can take several different forms, from a celebrity simply appearing in advertisements for a product, service or charity, to a celebrity attending PR events, creating his or her own line of products or services, and/or using his or her name as a brand.
- At present there has been a trend towards celebrity **voice-overs** in advertising. Some celebrities have distinct voices which are recognizable even when they not present on-screen. **Mr. Amitabh Bachchan** in Indian context is one such example. This is a more subtle way to add celebrity branding to a product or service.
- **Target Audience Receptivity.** In any celebrity endorsement deal proper match of the celebrity with the target audience profile is very essential to establish the right connects with the target audience.
- **Risk to Advertiser.** There has been a lot of instance of leading celebrities getting caught in **controversies** in their personal life. This is an important aspect that needs to be taken in to consideration and moral clause should be implemented to deal with this issue.

Beauty brands and fragrance houses have traditionally aligned themselves to celebrities. Sometimes that association surpasses the endorser's original claim to fame and we see an actress make headlines not for her craft but for her endorsement.

Celebrity endorsement is a costly proposition. It's a subject that never fails to stir debate. Hindi Film Stars earn enormous amount of money through brand endorsements. Most of the leading film stars from **Bollywood** are endorsing not just one but **multiple brands** in different product category and **globalization** has drawn major players from world over to explore the vast Indian market. Hence understanding and appreciating the **culture** of the Indian target audience is very essential to successfully operate in this country.

History

As per **Atkins and Block (1983)** a research on effectiveness of celebrity endorsement found that celebrities may be influential because celebrities are viewed as dynamic with both attractive and likeable qualities. In addition to this their name and fame is thought to attract attention to the product or service they are endorsing.

Another study by **Mc.Cracken (1989)** who is the Celebrity Endorser? Cultural Foundations of Endorsement process offer a new approach to celebrity endorsement. He criticized the **source credibility** and **source attractiveness** model and proposed the **meaning transfer model** as an alternative. The findings highlighted how meanings pass from celebrity to product and from product to consumer as per this model. The paper also mentions that according to this model the secret of celebrity endorsement is largely cultural in nature.

A study conducted by **Ohanian and Roobina (1990)** on construction and validation of a scale to measure celebrity endorsers' perceived Expertise, Trust worthiness and Attractiveness aimed at developing a scale for measuring celebrity endorsers' perceived expertise, trustworthiness, and attractiveness. Accepted **psychometric scale-development** procedures were followed which meticulously tested a large pool of items for their reliability and validity. Further, use of this scale can improve the understanding of how consumers in different situations react to different sources and how source credibility influences purchase intentions.

The study also revealed that since the large sums of money is spent on celebrity advertising, advertisers should use the scale as an integral part of their effectiveness testing and tracking. The scale is simple to use and convenient for large-sample administrations. For segmentation strategies, the wisdom of using a celebrity and the spokesperson's effectiveness for different demographic and psychographic consumer groups can be evaluated by applying this scale.

This concept also has applications beyond the use of celebrity spokespersons: the scale can be applied effectively in choosing the most appropriate "average consumer" as a spokesperson.

Finally, the dimensions of a celebrity endorser's credibility, along with consumer demographics and psychographics, can be used as potential predictors of attitude toward and intention to purchase a specific product.

As per Jagdish Agrawal & Wagner A. Kamakura (1995) a research on "The Economic worth of Celebrity Endorsers": An Event Study Analysis has typically focused on theories explaining how celebrity endorsements influence consumers' attitudes and intentions. The authors assess the impact of celebrity endorsement contracts on the expected profitability of a firm by using event study methodology.

The study also highlighted that Celebrity endorsement has become a prevalent form of advertising in the United States. Despite extensive literature on the effects of celebrity endorsements on consumers' brand attitudes and purchase intentions, little is known about the economic value of these endorsements.

The study revealed that the announcement of a celebrity endorsement contract, is usually widely made known in the business press, and is used as information by market analysts to evaluate the potential profitability of endorsement expenditures, thereby affecting the firm's expected return.

Announcements of 110 celebrity endorsement contracts were analyzed. Findings of the study indicate that, on average, the impact of these announcements on stock returns is positive and suggest that celebrity endorsement contracts are generally viewed as a worthwhile investment in advertising.

A study conducted by **Erdogan (1999) on** Celebrity Endorsement: A Literature Review focused how can companies select and retain the right' celebrity among many competing alternatives, and, simultaneously manage this resource, while avoiding potential pitfalls? This paper seeks to explore variables, which may be considered in any celebrity selection process. The study gave emphasis on **'Q'rating technique.**

This paper has identified factors from the academic literature which may have managerial importance for selecting celebrity endorsers. Notably, effectiveness of celebrity endorser is found to be moderated by several factors in the literature; celebrity attractiveness and credibility, product-celebrity match, message and product type, level of involvement number of endorsements by celebrities, target audience characteristics, and overall meanings (e.g. personality; values, standards) attached to celebrities.

Besides these factors, economic visibility of endorsers, regulative issues, compatibility with overall marketing strategy, and potential risks must be simultaneously also considered.

Mohan K. Menon et al.(2001) study on Celebrity Advertising: An assessment of its relative effectiveness examines difference between advertisement with celebrity and corresponding advertisement with non-celebrities. The paper in order to assess the relative effectiveness of celebrity advertisement, two types of advertising executions, Celebrity versus non-celebrity, were tested across print advertisement for six products: American Express, Apple Computers, Avon Cosmetics, Milk, Pepsi-Cola and Ray Ban Sunglasses. The sample comprised of students at south eastern University. Overall, the results from this study do not support the view that using celebrity advertisement is more believable or effective than non-celebrity advertisement for brands tested in this study.

According to **Sejung Marina Choi et al. (2005)** the study analyzed television commercials featuring celebrities from two different countries-the United States and Korea based on two different cultural dimensions. First **low versus high** context and secondly **individualism versus collectivism.** The findings highlighted that celebrities in the U.S advertisement's often **portrayed themselves** (i.e. they served as spokes person), while the majority of Korean celebrities acted in roles. Another interesting finding of the study was that many Korean celebrities appeared to promote more than one brand.

Though some research work on celebrity endorsement has been carried out in the United States and other western countries there is ample scope to explore this concept from different perspective especially in **Indian context**.

Globalization has added new dimension in the ways companies are trying to position their brand before the target audience and **celebrity advertising** is becoming very popular in India. This paper tried to explore the celebrity advertising phenomenon in **Indian cultural context.**

Scope and Significance

The phenomenon of celebrity endorsement is assuming increasing importance world wide. During the course of review of literature it was clearly evident that there is ample **scope** of exploring this issue in India with Indian celebrities (especially with **Hindi Film Stars** from **Bollywood**).In India celebrity endorsement is becoming very popular and companies are also trying to rope in leading Hindi Film Stars for endorsing their brands.

The **significance** of this study lies in the fact that it is aimed at identifying the **emerging trends** in celebrity advertising and determining the **challenges** faced by advertisers in connecting with the target audience of diverse cultural background and selecting a celebrity for brand endorsement and providing guidelines to them (**technique that may be adopted**) to help select the right celebrity because huge amount of money and other resources are at stake.

Study Objectives

The **objectives** of this research paper is to :

- **First** highlight the **emerging trends** noticed in marketing communication and celebrity advertising in India.
- **Secondly** identifying the **challenges** encountered by advertisers in regard to celebrity advertising.
- **Finally** under present Global scenario providing **strategic input** to advertisers in selecting the right celebrity to connect their brand with their target audience of diverse cultural background.

Celebrity Advertising – Challenges encountered in India

Selecting the right and appropriate celebrity for brand endorsement is really a challenging proposition. The various **dimensions of challenges** faced by the advertiser and their advertising agencies regarding celebrity selection in India may encompass the following aspects-

- Celebrity's fit with the brand image
- Celebrity Target Audience **cultural match**
- Celebrity's **familiarity** among the Target audience
- Celebrity's **popularity** among Target audience
- Cost associated with getting a celebrity
- Celebrity credibility
- Physical attractiveness
- Celebrity product match
- Celebrity's past endorsement history
- Celebrity endorsing Multiple Brands.

In Indian **cultural context** identifying the cultural parameters in respect to differences in **languages** of people of different region, **lifestyle** variations between people of different region, **value** systems, **norms and customs** followed by the people over the years and **ethics and moral standards** are to be appreciated and given due importance while developing a communication strategy.

Therefore identifying and selecting a **celebrity** who can connect with the target audience of diverse culture is a challenging proposition. This **research paper** is aimed at suggesting a technique called **"Q"score** to identify the most **familiar** and **popular celebrity** based on the findings of an empirical study in Kolkata.

Research Design

Exploratory study is conducted to get clarity of the objective by interacting with the respondents. Huge amount of money is spend on celebrity endorsement to reach the target audience belonging to different demographic profile therefore it is very important to find out the familiarity and popularity of the selected celebrities among the respondent.

First phase. Finding the **awareness and familiarity** of the 10 celebrities among different respondent group such as Students, Teachers, Business Men Housewife and respondent belonging to other occupations.

Second phase. In the second phase the **popularity** of the selected celebrities among the different respondent group was studied and with that overall ranking of the 10 celebrities were found out using 'Q' score technique.

Based on the study objectives mentioned above the research methodology comprised of both Primary Research and Secondary Research activities as mentioned below :

Secondary Research

A list of 10 Film Stars is prepared from the Hindi Film Industry in Mumbai who are endorsing multiple brands at present for the purpose of the study. Hindi Film Stars are selected for the study because of their huge **popularity and fan following** throughout the country.

After formulating the research problem, next the research design was framed. A research design is the conceptual structure within which the research is to be conducted- it deals with the collection, measurement and analysis of data.

Sample Design

Primary Research is conducted to find out the consumer's response regarding the study objectives discussed earlier.

Sample Size. A Sample size of **100** individuals, both **male** and **female** in the age group between **18-45** years belonging to different category such as **Students, Teacher, Businessmen, House wife etc**. is considered.

Sampling Type. Judgmental and Convenience sampling is done to select the respondents.

Data Collection

Data is collected by **Personal Interview Method** from the respondent in **Kolkata.**

Research Instrument used for the study was a structured **Questionnaire.**

Data analysis and Interpretation. Primary data collected during the course of the study is analyzed using simple percentages and **'Q' score** of the selected celebrities were found out to determine the familiarity and popularity of the selected celebrities.

Findings

The sample survey conducted in Kolkata to determine the **'Q' score** of the 10 selected celebrities bring to light some interesting findings.

The **study objective** relating to the **familiarity** of the celebrity among the respondents shows that all the **Hindi Film Stars** from Bollywood have 100% familiarity among the respondents.

Table 2. Familiarity score of celebrities (among 100 respondents)

Sr. No	*Celebrities (Name)*	*Number of Respondent Familiar*	*Percentage (%)*
1	Amitabh Bachchan	100	100
2	Shah Rukh Khan	100	100
3	Amir khan	100	100
4	Salman Khan	100	100
5	Hrithik Roshan	100	100
6	Saif Ali Khan	100	100
7	Rani Mukherjee	100	100
8	Preeti Zinta	100	100
9	Juhi Chawla	100	100
10	Aishwarya Rai Bachchan	100	100

Findings' regarding the **study objective** relating to **popularity** of the celebrities among the respondents shows that among all the **Hindi Film Stars Amitabh Bachchan** and **Shah Rukh Khan** both are having the maximum popularity **(47%)** followed by Amir Khan (41%), Rani Mukherjee (38%), Hrithik Roshan (33%), Salman Khan (20%), Aishwarya Rai Bachchan (19%), Preeti Zinta (17%), Juhi Chawla (12%) and Saif Ali Khan (11%) is having the least popularity among the film stars.

Table 3 Popularity score of celebrities (among 100 respondents)

Sr. No	*Celebrities (Name)*	*Number of Respondent*	*Percentage (%)*
1	Amitabh Bachchan	47	47
2	Shah Rukh Khan	47	47
3	Amir khan	41	41
4	Salman Khan	20	20
5	Hrithik Roshan	33	33
6	Saif Ali Khan	11	11
7	Rani Mukherjee	38	38
8	Preeti Zinta	17	17
9	Juhi Chawla	12	12
10	Aishwarya Rai Bachchan	19	19

Findings regarding the **final study objective** clearly bring to light the **'Q' score** of the **10 Indian Celebrities**. Among all the selected celebrities **Amitabh Bachchan and Shah Rukh Khan** are both having the **highest 'Q' score (47)** followed by **Amir Khan (41), Rani Mukherjee (38) etc.**

Table 4 showing the familiarity score, popularity score & 'Q' score of the celebrities (Total number of respondents 100)

Sr. No.	Celebrities	Familiarity Score	Familiarity Percentage (%)	Popularity score	Popularity Percentage (%)	'Q' Score
1	Amitabh Bachchan	100	100	47	47	47
2	Shah Rukh Khan	100	100	47	47	47
3	Amir khan	100	100	41	41	41
4	Salman Khan	100	100	20	20	20
5	Hrithik Roshan	100	100	33	33	33
6	Saif Ali Khan	100	100	11	11	11
7	Rani Mukherjee	100	100	38	38	38
8	Preeti Zinta	100	100	17	17	17
9	Juhi Chawla	100	100	12	12	12
10	Aishwarya Rai Bachchan	100	100	19	19	19

Finally based on the **'Q' score** overall **ranking** of the 10 celebrities is done and **Amitabh Bachchan and Shah Rukh Khan** emerged as the top most celebrity (**rank1**) followed by Amir Khan (rank 3) and Rani Mukherjee in 4th place and Saif Ali Khan is having the lowest rank.

Table 5 (Showing the Ranking of the celebrities based on their 'Q' Score)

Celebrities	'Q' Score	Ranking
Amitabh Bachchan	**47**	**1**
Shah Rukh Khan	**47**	**1**

Amir khan	41	3
Rani Mukherjee	38	4
Hrithik Roshan	33	5
Salman Khan	20	6
Aishwarya Rai Bachchan	19	7
Preeti Zinta	17	8
Juhi Chawla	12	9
Saif Ali Khan	11	10

Limitation & Scope for Further Research

This study has got some limitations as mentioned below. The study is conducted with a sample of 100 respondents in Kolkata only and for the study only 10 Indian celebrities (**Hindi Film Stars**) were selected.

The study gives a clear direction for **future research** in this aspect of understanding the celebrity advertising phenomenon in India under Globalization and measuring the familiarity and popularity of Indian celebrities in a much broader manner with celebrities from other walks of life and among larger sample size covering much broader geographic area.

Conclusion

This research paper was aimed at gaining an insight about the phenomenon of celebrity advertising in India keeping the **diverse culture** in mind. The paper also highlighted the **emerging trends** noticed in celebrity advertising in India in regard to **multiple brand endorsement, celebrity branding etc.** It also determined the different **dimension of challenges** faced by advertisers in selecting a celebrity for brand endorsement to connect with the target audience belonging to diverse cultural background.

The techniques and concepts suggested in the paper clearly give an indication to the advertisers about how to overcome the challenges involved in celebrity selection for brand endorsement.

The paper focused on some key objectives regarding determining the **familiarity and popularity of Indian celebrities** because they are endorsing different brands and occupying huge amount of advertising space and time across different mass media.

The findings that emerged from the study throw a lot of light regarding the **familiarity and popularity** of the celebrities among respondents belonging to different demographic profile.

Mr.Amitabh Bachchan & Mr. Shah Rukh Khan emerged as the most popular celebrities with the highest "Q" score and **Saif Ali Khan** is rated as the least preferred celebrity having the lowest "Q" score.

The study also gives a clear indication to leading companies and their advertising agencies regarding the **'Q' score** of the 10 selected celebrities which can be used as a **guideline** to select the appropriate celebrity for endorsing their brand to reach their target audience especially in Indian context.

Reference

Atkin, Charles and Martin Block,. Effectiveness of Celebrity Endorsers. Journal of Advertising Research 23, 1 (February/March 1983): 57-62.

Belch & Belch, Advertising and Promotion: An Integrated Marketing

Communication Perspective, Using 'Q' scores and the fame index to help choose a celebrity endorser. Sixth edition, Tata Mc.Graw-Hill, 2003, pp 178-179.

"Celebrity endorsement ads on TV up 49% during 2007", Business Line April 09, 2008, http://www.blonnet.com/2008/04/09/stories/2008040950750500.htm

Choi, Sejung Marina, Wei-Na Lee, and Hee-jung Kim (2005), "Lessons from the Rich and Famous: A Cross-Cultural Comparisons of Celebrity Endorsement in Advertising," Journal of Advertising, 34 (2), 85-98.

Erdogan, B. Zafar (1999), "Celebrity Endorsement: A Literature Review," Journal of Marketing Management, 15, 291-314.

Jagdish Agrawal & Wagner A. Kamakura, The Economic Worth of Celebrity Endorsers: An Event Study Analysis Journal of Marketing Vol. 59 (July 1995), 56-62

Kamins, Michael A, Meribeth J. Brand, Stuart A. Hoeke, and John C. Moe, Two-Sided Versus One-Sided Celebrity Endorsements: The Impact on Advertising Effectiveness and Credibility.Journal of Advertising 18, no. 2 (1989): 4-10.

Mala Tandon & Sudeep Mehrotra "Impact of Celebrity Endorsements on Overall Brand" http://www.coolavenues.com/know/mktg/sudeep1.php

McCracken, Grant, Who is the Celebrity Endorser? Cultural Foundations of the Endorsement Process. Journal of Consumer Research 16, (December 1989):310-32 1.

Mohan K. Menon and Louis E. Boone and Hudson P. Rogers, **Celebrity Advertising: An Assessment of Its Relative Effectiveness, SMA conference, 2001**

Ohanian, Roobina, Construction and Validation of a Scale to Measure Celebrity Endorsers' Perceived Expertise, Trustworthiness, and Attractiveness. Journal of Advertising 19, (1990): 39 – 52

Shimp, T. E. (1997), Advertising. Promotion and Supplemental Aspects of Integrated Marketing Communication, 4th Edition. Fort Worth, Texas: The Dryden Press.

Solomon, Michael R (1996), Consumer Behavior. 3rd Edition, London: Prentice-Hall International, Inc

Tripp, Carolyn, Thomas D.Jensen, and Les Carlson, "The Effect of Multiple Product Endorsement by Celebrities on Consumer Attitudes and Intentions," Journal of Consumer research, 20(4), (1994): 535-547

Communication Challenges in International Milieu

INTRODUCTION

Communication is a social process by which messages are exchanged between people through a common set of symbols. In today's competitive business environment due to economic liberation and globalization various multinational companies having varied cultural backgrounds are coming closer for commercial purposes. Communication being the lifeline of any organization, it has become imperative for professional to understand the cultural differences in intercultural communication. Culture refers to the behavioral characteristics typical to the group which are reflected through their verbal and non verbal communication within that group. It consists of many aspects such as religion, language, rituals, dress, traditions, values, interest, food habits, etc. Differences in cultural values and perception can be an invisible source of great misunderstanding between people from different cultural backgrounds. A poor understanding in areas such as languages, etiquette, non-verbal communication, norms and values may lead to damaging blunders. On the other hand an understanding of cultural differences will pave way for effective communication at various work places.

With the main objective of understanding cultural differences and their subsequent impact on communication process, this paper at the outset elaborates the term culture and then moves on to discuss the various cultural differences which may cause lapses in communication. The paper also suggests some measures to minimize lapses caused by cultural differences.

Developing excellent **communication skills** is extremely important. Survey of employees often shows that communication skills are critical to effective job placement, performance career advancement, and organizational success. In making hiring decisions, employers often rank communication skills among the most – requested competencies. In fact, many job advertisements specifically ask for excellent oral and written communication skills.

Now in this 21st century, the phenomenal growth of internal trade creates the need to understand intercultural communication – the ability to speak and write in ways that are sensitive to and cognizant of the factors in different cultural contexts. Organizational Communication is influenced by various factors amongst which the context in which it occurs is very important. The overwhelming influence of culture on communication led famous anthropologist Edward Hall to assert, "Culture is communication and communication is culture". We all communicate with others all the time – in our homes, in our workplaces, in the groups we belong to, and in the community.

Key Words: *Intercultural, Etiquette, Non-verbal, Rituals*

No matter how well we think we understand each other, communication is difficult. Just think, for example, how often we hear things like, "He doesn't get it," or "She didn't really hear what I meant to say." "Culture" is often at the root of communication challenges. Our culture influences how we approach problems, and how we participate in groups and in communities.

Undoubtedly, it is more comfortable to work with persons of our own culture, our own language, and our own communication norms. But international communication demands work with many foreign countries and people. The workplace environment includes employees and customers with a wide range of needs, interest, abilities, and culture backgrounds. If culture diversity is not understood and valued, misunderstandings may occur that negatively affect business success.

To overcome this problem and to mitigate the effect at global level this paper has come up with some finding that would enhance competence in language use so that intercultural communication is strengthened.

With its main objective of understanding the chief communication challenges in international milieu, this paper at the outset elaborates the term culture and throws some light on intercultural communication model. Then it moves on to discuss the various cultural variables that exist at the national and the individual levels. Apart from this, a sincere effort has been made to explain the barriers arising out of ethnocentrism and cultural relativism. Finally, the paper also extends some valuable suggestions to mitigate various communication challenges arising out of cultural diversity.

A Concept of Culture

Culture is a complex concept, with legion of definitions. But, according to the dictionary the word, "culture" refers to a group or community with which we share common experiences that shape the way we understand the world. It includes groups that we are born into, such as gender, race, or national origin. It also includes groups we join or become part of. For example, we can acquire a new culture by moving to a new region, by a change in our economic status, or by becoming disabled. Simply we can define culture in this way.

"A culture is a communication of learned behavior and results of behavior whose component elements are shared and transmitted by the members of particular society".

There is no doubt as to the many cultural groups around the world with different patterns of behavior, values and rules. These conventions are culture specific i.e. different cultures develop different rules for achieving the same task and people attach different meanings to the same events. The same action is thus evaluated in different terms for example, thumbs up in America means approval, but in Iran and Ghana it is a vulgar gesture. Similarly if people stand too close when conversing, Germans, Canadians, and Americans may feel uncomfortable; in Middle Eastern cultures, however, conversations may be almost nose to nose.

Cultural Relativism and Ethnocentrism

Cultural relativism compares the values and behaviors of different cultures and usually means judging them against standards of right and wrong for our own culture. This approach to other cultures becomes a barrier when we assume that cultural beliefs, values, and behaviors are wrong if they differ from those of our own culture. Ethnocentrism is the inherent belief that our own cultural traditions and values are correct and superior. This natural attitude is found in all cultures. Ethnocentrism causes us to judge others by our own values. If a person was raised in North America, the values just described probably seem "right" to him or her. That person may wonder why the rest of the world does not function in the same sensible fashion .People around the world are ethnocentric to a degree. Beliefs, values, and behaviors that differ from those of our culture may seem peculiar, strange, and even wrong. However, as a person study different cultures recognize that there is not just one right or wrong way but that different ways can be equally correct. Some very simple examples of ethnocentric thinking – we often talk about British drivers driving "on the wrong side" of the road. Why not just say "opposite side" or even "left hand side"? We talk about written Hebrew as reading "backwards". Why not just say "from right to left" or "in the opposite direction from English." An Arab considers a North American who wants to set a deadline for completion of negotiation pushy. That same Arab, who prefers a handshake to written contract, is seen as native and possibly untrustworthy by a North American.

Cultural Variables

When most people use the word culture they think of people from different national backgrounds. National cultures certainly do exist and play an important role in shaping the way people communicate. But there are other dimensions of culture too. Within a nation, regional differences can exert a powerful influence on communication. Race, ethnicity, customs, values, attitudes can shape behavior. Gender, sexual orientation, physical disabilities, religion, socio-economic backgrounds are just a few. Broadly we can divide the cultural variables into two categories.

National Cultural Variables

Both the message sender and the receiver are affected by external and internal stimuli. When communicating with business people in a foreign country, people must realize that overall national and individual cultural differences within the cultures further affect those stimuli. The national and individual constraints and variables that communicators face when working with foreign receivers of their messages have been discussed below.

Religion. In the United States people accept religious diversity; they are tolerant of Protestant, Catholic, Jewish, Buddhist, Hindu, Moslem, and many other personal beliefs. Other foreign countries are less tolerant. For instance Iran is less tolerant of diversity in religion.

In connection with religion there is great need for tolerance. Buddhism, Hinduism, and Moslem religions are found in many parts of the world, affecting the values (and attire) of people. For instance, theses three religions forbid consumption of alcohol; thus no liquor is served at business affairs. To communicate well internationally, it is also essential to understand the diversity patterns within one's own country.

Language. An important constraint that under girds all the preceding variables is language. Obviously, unless both sender and receiver understand a common language, the opportunities for successful business communication are significantly limited. Unfortunately, wide differences among languages make precisely equivalent translation difficult. One reason for differences is that languages are based on the concepts, experiences, views, and such of the cultures that developed them. Different cultures have different concepts, experiences, views, and such. For example, we think of a florist as someone who sells flowers and related items in a store. In some cultures, however, flowers are sold by street venders, mainly women and children. Obviously, English word "florist" does not have a precise equivalent in the language of such cultures. Similarly, English word "supermarket" has no equivalent in some languages. Advertising language must also be analyzed for its cultural suitability. For example, the slogan employed by the computer games manufacturer, EA Sports, "Challenge Everything" raises grumbles of disapproval in religious or hierarchical societies where harmonious relationships are maintained through the values of respect and non-confrontation.

Similarly it was reported that in the early 1950s, an American ink manufacturer attempted to sell bottled ink in Mexico while its metal outdoor signs told customers that they could "avoid embarrassment' (from leaks and stains) by using its brand of ink. The embarrassment, it sees was all the ink company's. The Spanish word used to convey the meaning of "embarrassed' was "embarazar,' which means "to become pregnant.' Many people thought the company was selling contraceptive device. It is imperative therefore that language be examined carefully in any cross cultural advertising campaign. Overcoming such language problems is difficult. The best way, of course, is to know more than one language.

Economics. Availability of capital and transportation and the standard of living per capital vary from nation to nation. The opportunity to borrow money, the rate of inflation, and the exchange rates influence business and a county's ability to communicate concerning that business. Under the U.S. free – enterprise system, competitors usually set their own prices. In contrast, OPEC (organization of Petroleum Exporting Countries), as a cartel, sets oil prices. Israeli agricultural, competitors mutually agree on a price. Some Japanese businesses check with the government before initiating major production and trading changes. And only recently have freedom associated with capitalism made inroads in Eastern Europe and the southern part of China.

Education. It may be wrong on our part to think that educational systems of all nations are alike. For example the way in which the universities and colleges function may be different in different countries. The curriculum, teaching methodology, evaluation systems, etc., differ. Also the emphasis given to various degree programs varies across the nations. Few major schools in Germany offer classes in business or managerial communication. Often training occurs outside the university, in private and public seminars frequently taught by non-academics. But in India most of the business schools include this course in their curriculum. Similarly the amount of interaction between universities and the industries may not be the same. The education may be formal or informal and it may depend upon the nation's history and social development. These factors need to be understood thoroughly if we wish to communicate globally for our business purposes.

Politics. The type of government and even the concept of democracy vary from nation to nation. Also the sweeping political changes in a nation may affect the way businesses are run there. The political stability and instability of the nation in which we wish to conduct our business or communicate for our business, need to be monitored. All such events affect communication, understanding of a country, and a company's willingness to do business in an unclear political environment.

Individual Cultural Variables

In the preceding section we have discussed the macro national characteristics affecting communication- both intra-national and international. The forthcoming section throws some light up on the individual variables-variables related to the unique lifestyle of personal habits and ethnic diversity. Thus, within each culture, on the micro and more personal level, are differences in verbal and non-verbal cues expressed through varying concept of time, individual speech, food, acceptable dress, manners at home and at work, decision-making patterns, and other nonverbal variations.

Time. In American culture people are very punctual. They try their best to meet the deadline as it's essential for the smooth conduction of the business. Quite contrary to it in most of the Asian courtiers people view time in more relaxed way. They see planning as unwise and unnecessary. Various organizations in the United States such as business, government, and schools – keep time by the calendar and the clock. Other cultures may keep time by the sessions and the moon, the sun, internal "body clocks", or a personal feeling that "the time is right."

Space. Personal space is the distance someone wants between himself or herself. Most North Americans, North Europeans, and Asian want a bigger personal space than do Latin American, French, Italians, and Arabs. Even within a culture, some people like more personal space than do others. One U. S. study found that men took more personal space than women did.

Eye contact. North American whites see eye contact as a sign of honesty. But in many cultures, dropped eyes are a sign of appropriate deference to a superior. Puerto Rican children are taught not to meet the eyes of adults. The Japanese are taught to look at the neck. In Korea, prolonged eye contact is considered rude. The lower - ranking person is expected to look down first. In Muslim countries, women and men are not supposed to have eye contact. These differences can lead to miscommunication in the multicultural workplace. Superior may feel that subordinates are being disrespectful when the subordinates are being fully respectful- according to the norms of his or her culture.

Values, Beliefs, and Practices. Values and beliefs, often unconscious, affect a person's response to people and situations. Most North Americans accept competition and believe that it produces better performance. The Japanese, however, believe that competition leads to disharmony. U.S. business people believe that success is based on individual achievement and is open to anyone who excels. In England and in France, success is more obviously linked to social class. And in some countries, people of some caste or races are prohibited by law from full participation in society.

Many people in the United States value individualism. Other countries may value the group. In traditional classrooms, U.S. students are expected to complete assignments alone; if they get much help from anyone else, they're "cheating". In contrast, groups routinely work together to solve problems in Japan. In the dominant U.S. culture, quiet is a sign that people are working. In Japan people talk to get the work done. These differences in values, beliefs, and practices lead to differences in what kinds of appeals motivate people..

Non verbal communication. In multicultural business communication, non verbal signals vary as much as spoken languages do. Non verbal greetings vary from a bow to a handshake or from a hug to an upward flick of the eyebrows. Not understanding cultural differences in nonverbal messages causes communication problems. For example, the Japanese consider crossing one's legs by placing one foot or ankle on the knee of the other leg to be impolite or vulgar. The preferred way of sitting is with both feet on the floor with knees together. Thumbs up in America means approval, but in Iran and Ghana it is a vulgar gesture. In addition, the social distance or individual space that persons need for comfort in communication varies in different cultures. If people stand too close when conversing, Germans, Canadians, and Americans may feel uncomfortable; in Middle Eastern cultures, however, conversations may be almost nose to nose.

Decision making. Indians and Japanese believe in group decision making while Americans and Germans believe in individual decision making. Participation, by many people, is the touchstone. Though we believe in group decision making, as Indians, we can very well realize that the time taken to arrive at a decision or complete a project undertaken by the governmental agencies may even cross decade at times. Much time is spent in reaching an answer. That is what frustrates Americans; that is where they throw up their hands. Thus patience and our understanding of the decision process- add to of our success in dealing with a foreign environment.

Guidelines for Intercultural Communication

We live in an increasingly complex world. One element of this complexity is the mixing of different cultures, languages and faiths. Within the business world intercultural communication is vital for success. Effective communication between colleagues from different cultural backgrounds ensures a team is working harmoniously. A person can become an effective multicultural communicator if he/she follows a few simple guidelines. Understanding our own culture, keeping an open mind and respecting differences , adapting to cultural communication patterns, and identifying language differences can improve multicultural interactions. The guidelines to intercultural communication are basic pointers that all working in intercultural teams should be aware of to ensure culture becomes a vehicle for positive advancement rather than a barrier.

Respect Diversity. Learn about other cultures, beliefs, and customs without judging them by our own cultural identity and unexamined biases. This is not to suggest that people should change their beliefs or disrespects their own culture, but rather that they should recognize that cultural values affect beliefs and behaviors and that understanding how others interpret verbal and nonverbal language helps them in receiving the intended response. However, avoid accepting stereotypes that assume that characteristics that may apply to some people in a particular culture are characteristic of all individuals in that culture. Knowledge of an individual's ethnic or other cultural background is only an initial clue to understand his or her interests, needs, and values.

Learn language differences. While communicating with persons from another culture, people should learn how that culture's verbal and nonverbal languages differ from our own culture. Observe and learn the meaning of nonverbal communication signals such as facial expressions, social distance for conversing, and hand gestures. Avoid non verbal signals that may be offensive. When speaking or writing, alter language and change traditional word usage to avoid language that offends someone. Be sensitive and considerate of other's beliefs.

Break Assumptions. Everyone makes or has assumptions about others. Assumptions are beliefs rather than objective truth and are usually influenced by a number of subjective factors. For intercultural communication to truly work, people need to assess their assumptions and ask themselves why they hold those ideas or beliefs. By doing so and even openly examining them with others, the initial barrier to intercultural communication is overcome.

Empathize. In order to come to appreciate and understand people from different cultures, empathy is vital. Through putting our self in someone else's shoes we come to see or appreciate their point of view.

Discourage Herd Mentality. Herd mentality refers to a closed and one dimensional approach. Such a way of thinking curbs creativity, innovation and advancement as people is restricted in how to think approach and engage with people or challenges. Intercultural communication can only flourish and therefore contribute if people are encouraged to think as individuals, bring their cultural influences to the table and share ideas that may be outside the box.

Summary

Intercultural communication today means getting an edge as today business is highly competitive and fast changing. It is crucial for today's business personnel to understand the impact of intercultural differences on business, trade and internal company organization. The success or failure of a company, venture, merger or acquisition is essentially in the hands of people. If these people are not aware of different cultures then misunderstandings, offence and a break down in communication can occur. Basic to any country are certain national variables such as education, politics, language, religion etc. These mega principles indirectly affect a nation's population. Similarly within each country there are individual people – all with their own personal behaviors involving how they handle time, what a comfortable distance for interpersonal communication is, what is considered appropriate dress, what procedures and speed are followed in arriving at personal and business decisions. Each of them influences the course of communications, and can be responsible for conflict or the escalation of conflict when it leads to miscommunication or misinterpretation. A culturally-fluent approach to conflict means working over time to understand these and other ways communication varies across cultures, and applying these understandings in order to enhance relationships across differences. Successful intercultural communication requires enthusiasm and a willingness to overcome cultural barriers. It is a two -way process.

References

1. Mary L. Tucker and Anne M. McCarthy, "Presentation Self-Efficacy: Increasing Communication Skills Through Service – Learning," Journals of Managerial Issues, Summer 2001, 227-244.
2. W.J. Wilhelm, "A Delphi Study of Entry- Level Workplace Skills, Competencies, and Proof- of- Achievement Products," The Delta Pi Epsilon Journal, 1999, 41, 105-122.
3. Janette Moody, Brent Stewart, and Cynthia Bolt – Lee, Showcasing the Skilled Business Graduate: Expanding the Tool Kit," Business Communication Quarterly, March 2002, 23.
4. Murphy Herta A., Herbert W. Hildebrandt, Jane P. Thomas, Effective Business Communication 7th ed. McGrew – Hill, New York.1997, 70-83.
5. Raman Meenakshi, Culture Communication and Work ,In: Communicating at Work Shifting paradigms and Emerging Trends.(Meenakshi R., Sangeeta S. , Binod M., Eds.), Jain Brothers, New Delhi, India.2005,273-288.
6. E. Marcelle, DuPraw and Marya Axner, Working on Common Cross-cultural Communication Challenges. [Cited 2009 June 15] Available from: www.pbs.org/ampu/crosscult.html
7. Krizan A.C. " Buddy" , Patricia M., Joyce L, Karen W., Business Communication 7th ed. Baba Barkha Nath printers , Haryana , India. 2008, 24-34.

8. Linton, R. The Cultural Background of Personality. New York. 1945 ,32.
9. Patrice Simpson, Intercultural Communication.[cited 2009 may 16] Available from: www.ptc.nsw.edu.au/scansw/intcultsimpson.html
10. Guffey Mary Ellen, Essentials of Business Communication 6th ed. Melissa Acuna , Ohio, USA.2004,12- 13.
11. Flatley Lesikar, Business Communication 9th ed. McGrew-Hill, New Delhi, India. 2002, 437-446.
12. **International Advertising: Understanding Cultural Differences**.[cited 2009 June 28]
    Available from: www.sideroad.com/...Cultural.../international-advertising.html
13. Jonathan R. Slater. April 1984 [cited 2009 June 27]
    Available from: findarticles.com/p/articles/mi_m1052/is_v7/ai_3210962
14. Locker Kitty O, Stephen Kyo Kaczmarek, Business Communication, 3rd ed. McGrew – Hill, New Delhi, India.2007,40-47.
15. Payne Neil, **Breaking the Barriers of Intercultural Communication**. [Cited 2009 may 12]
    Available from www.sideroad.com/...Communication/barrier-of-intercultural-communication.html

Expectations and Opinions of the Farmers Towards ICT in Agriculture

INTRODUCTION

The economy of our nation is based on agriculture and allied agro based industries, animal husbandry and other agriculture based businesses. Agriculture continues to be the major occupation and way of life for more than half of the total population. Thus, overall development of our country is not possible by ignoring the agriculture and farmers in the process of development. Since major segment of our population are being lived in the rural areas, quick dissemination of technology information from the agriculture research system to the doorstep of the ultimate users and reporting their problems to research system are the critical inputs in transfer of agricultural technology. It is observed that the information and communication support during last few decades has mainly been conventional. This approach has not been able to reach large mass of the farmers who are spread across the whole country.

Amongst the various means for information communication are available, satellite based internet communication found very efficient, accurate, quick and somewhat cheaper in the field of disseminating the information from research system to farmers. Internet communication has touched almost all the district in our country and is mainly down up to the village levels. Internet offers a means for bridging the gap between developmental professional, rural people and agricultural producers through the initiation of interaction and dialogue.

Keeping all the views in mind it was decided to study the expectations and opinion of the farmers regarding internet facility with the following specific objectives.

(1) To study the expectations and opinion of the farmers towards internet facility

(2) To ascertain the relationship between personal profile and opinion of the farmers towards internet facility

The objective of the study was to know the expectations and opinion of the farmers regarding Community Internet Center at village level for sustainable agricultural development. Most of the respondents was expected the Community Internet Center (CIC) facilities at panchayat office of the village . They were also expecting six sets of computer with agriculture graduate having computer knowledge as operator at CIC. They expect that Government should bear expenses to run CIC. The information on farmers' related sites was expected by most of the farmers in Gujarati language that too in the audio-visual form. The major purposes to have CIC explained by the respondents were to collect agricultural information, to collect information on government's programmes, and to know more about market prices. Majority of the respondents expressed their desire to use Internet daily or twice in a week by their own .All of them expressed positive response to have proper training about the use of Internet facility through government agency, at CIC. The results showed that majority of the farmers understood that internet is a rich source to collect world wide information on agriculture and it is the fastest way to exchange information in shortest time'. Majority farmers completely or to a certain degree felt that though internet is costly affair for the farmers but it is the best mean to collect information on market prices of agricultural products. 82.00 percent of the farmers were wishing their children to make positive use of internet at the same time 81.00 per cent of them had opinion that farmers should make use of internet.

It can be concluded from the results that out of the 10 independent variables, five variables like Education, Land holding, Contact with NRI's, Experience of internet use and Mass media exposure are significantly and positively correlated with the opinion of the farmers about the use of Internet for farming community. More than 70 per cent of the farmers opined that internet is the rich source and fastest way of exchanging information in short time. It must be use by the farming community for their betterment.

Farmers are more desirous and become anxious to get quick, exact and authentic information in the changing scenario of agriculture at global level. Dissemination of the required and recent agricultural information to the farmers in scattered villages at the variegated geographical situation in India is very difficult task.

Transfer of technology to the level of farmers is not a one time exercise because new farm technology is being constantly evolved. A continuous flow of technologies in an appropriate manner is vital to provide quick benefit of this development to the farmers. There has been a technological explosion in the field of agriculture. This demands that the farmer has to know all aspects of technology prior to its adoption. It can only be possible through the use of satellite based Internet technologies.

Agriculture continues to be the major occupation and way of life for more than half of the total population. Thus, overall development of our country is not possible by ignoring the agriculture and farmers in the process of development. Since major segment of our population are being lived in the rural areas, quick dissemination of technology information from the agriculture research system to the doorstep of the ultimate users and reporting their problems to research system are the critical inputs in transfer of agricultural technology. It is observed that the information and communication support during last few decades has mainly been conventional. Amongst the various means for information communication are available, satellite based internet communication found very efficient, accurate, quick and somewhat cheaper in the field of disseminating the information from research system to farmers. Internet communication has touched almost all the district in our country and is mainly down up to the village levels. Internet offers a means for bridging the gap between developmental professional, rural people and agricultural producers through the initiation of interaction and dialogue.

The number of satellite based Internet connection in Indian has crossed the two million mark and the number of telephone connections is over 320 million. Internet connectivity has touched almost all the districts in the country and is moving down up to the village levels (Aditya,2003). Many pilot projects to connect rural community to cyber-space are underway at various locations. The initial response of the rural people, particularly farmers has been very encouraging; many organizations are trying to establish internet connectivity to make best use to satellite based communication technology. Keeping all the things in mind the present study has been undertaken with a view to know the Expectations of the farmers regarding Community Internet Centre (CIC) at village level as well as to study entitled opinion of the farmers regarding internet facility was carried out in Anand district of Gujarat state. Four village having more than 5000 population and comparatively sound infrastructure facilities were selected purposively. A list of progressive farmers was prepared with the help of village level worker from all the selected villages. Finally, 25 farmers were selected from each villages using simple random sampling technique. Thus, the study was confined to 100 farmers.

The results revealed that most of the respondents was expected the Community Internet Center (CIC) facilities at panchayat office of the village. They were also expecting six sets of computer with agriculture graduate having computer knowledge as operator at CIC. They expect that Government should bear expenses to run CIC. The information on farmers' related sites was expected by most of the farmers in Gujarati language that too in the audio-visual form. The major purposes to have CIC explained by the respondents were to collect agricultural information, to collect information on government's programmes, and to know more about market prices. Majority of the respondents expressed their desire to use Internet daily or twice in a week by their own .All of them expressed positive response to have proper training about the use of Internet facility through government agency, at CIC.

The results showed that majority of the farmers understood that internet is a rich source to collect world wide information on agriculture and it is the fastest way to exchange information in shortest time'. Majority farmers completely or to a certain degree felt that though internet is costly affair for the farmers but it is the best mean to collect information on market prices of agricultural products. 82.00 percent of the farmers were wishing their children to make positive use of internet at the same time 81.00 per cent of them had opinion that farmers should make use of internet.

Out of the 10 independent variables, five variables like Education, Land holding, Contact with NRI's, Experience of internet use and Mass media exposure were observed positively significant while, remaining five variables such as type of the family was observed negatively significant with the opinion of the farmers about the use of Internet for farming community. The independent variables like Age, Occupation, Animal wealth, Modern agricultural equipment, Type of family, Extension contact and Organization participation were observed non significant with the opinion of the farmers about the use of Internet for farming community.

Methodology

The investigation was carried out in Anand district of Gujarat state because the district is agriculturally one of the more advanced districts. Farmers having good interaction with their relatives in foreign countries. Four villages Viz. Vasad, Mogar, Napad and Navli having more than 5000 population and comparatively sound infrastructure facilities were selected purposively. A list of progressive farmers was prepared with the help of village level worker from all the selected villages. Finally, 25 farmers were selected from each villages using simple random sampling technique. Thus, the study was confined to 100 farmers. Keeping in view the objectives of the study, data were collected using structured interview schedule prepared for the purpose. Statistical tools such as frequency and percent and co-efficient of correlation were employed to analyze the data.

Results and Discussion

Profile of the respondents

It was observed that 64 per cent of the internet facility expecting farmers were from the middle age group, with a high school and higher secondary level of education (45 per cent) and had joint family. Sixty percent of the respondents belonged to the small category of farmers with mixed farming as main occupation. In order to earn additional income along with farming about 46 per cent of them possessed two or more animals. More than half of the respondents were found to be the member in one or more organizations.

Expectation of the farmers about CIC

The data presented in Table 1 indicates that cent percent of the respondents expected to have CIC at village level. It shows that farmers have realized importance of Internet facility in villages as an effective source of information as well as for the speedy communication.

It can be observed from the data in table 2 that Building of Panchayat was preferred by 95.00 per cent of the respondents, followed by building of primary school by 81.00 per cent, building of co-operative dairy by 76.00 per cent and buildings of high school and community hall by only 5.00 and 3.00 percent respondents, respectively. The building of panchayat is such an informal place, where people feel much familiarity, thus it was preferred by great majority of the farmers to have CIC.The data in Table 3 indicate that operator or guide, printer, separate cabin, downloaded information in printed form and extra seating facilities were expected by 98.00, 72.00, 68.00, 63.00 and 53.00 per cent of the farmers, respectively. The data in Table 4 indicate that agriculture graduate with computer knowledge was preferred by nearly cent per cent (98.00 per cent) of the farmers as a manager of the centre, followed by any educated person of the village was preferred by 76.00 per cent, expert of computer by 57.00 per cent and primary school teacher by 28.00 per cent of the farmers.

With a view to knowing farmers' choice of source to take initial financial support to start CIC, information was collected and presented in Table 5. The first choice of the farmers to take initial financial support to start CIC was Government agencies followed by co-operative societies, villagers sharing, voluntary donation and foreign relatives.

The information regarding choice of the farmers to bear expenses to run CIC was also collected and presented in Table 6. It can be seen that respondents said that Government should bear expenses to run CIC, at the same time other preferences given by them to bear expenses to run CIC were village panchayat, co-operative dairy and collecting charges from users.

Respondents were also asked to give there expectation regarding number of internet connected sets of computers(Table 7). Majority of the farmers (78 per cent) suggested that more than six sets should be there at CIC while 22.oo per cent expected 5 to 6 sets of internet connected computer sets at CIC.

It can be seen from Table-8 that most of the farmers was expected information in Gujarati language that too in the form of photographs and written form on agricultural related webs as well as on ICT. At the initial stage if it is difficult to provide information on most expected form, thus many of them were also expected information in audio-visual form, written form and audio form.

The data presented in Table 9 reveals that the major uses of internet expected by the respondents were to collect agricultural information, to collect information on government's programmes, for speedy communication, for exchange information, for entertainment, to collect information for their children's education, to contact foreign relatives, to contact relatives in India, to know information on agriculture of developed county and to know more about market prices (Buddhadev, 2003). The farmers are ready to use Internet for agricultural information but on majority of the agricultural sites, information is available in English language so they are not in opposition to use it. Thus, all State Government should launch farmers' related sites in local languages. Many State Governments have initiated their efforts in this direction

The result Table 10 shows that farmers have real interest to be a part of Internet communication process thus, majority (78.00 per cent) of the respondents were expecting to use

Internet by their own while, 22.00 per cent were wanted to use it with the help of others.

The expected frequency of the farmers to use Internet facility at CIC was measure. The result (Table 11) indicates that majority (63.00 per cent) of respondent were expecting to use internet at CIC daily or twice in a week, followed by 28 per cent whenever needed, 06.00 per cent once in a week and 3.00 per cent once in a fortnight. Thus it can be said that favorable expectation was observed among the farmers to use Internet at CIC. The data presented in Table 12 indicate that majority (70.00 per cent) of respondents expected training through government agency, followed by 13.00 per cent expected training by Agricultural University, 11.00 per cent respondents by Gram Panchayat. Only 4.00 and 2.00 percent of them expected such training by co-operative society and NGOs.

The data presented in Table 13 indicated that 71.00 per cent of the farmers understood that internet is a rich source to collect world wide information on agriculture and its allied fields, while 72.00 per cent supported to the statement that 'Internet is fastest way to exchange information in shortest time'. Looking to the present cost involved in this technology, it is not easy for the farmers to have this facility individually at his home, thus, 65.00 per cent of the farmers completely or to a certain degree felt that internet is costly affair for the farmers. Internet is best mean to collect information on market prizes of agricultural products but as it is being new system for our farmers, mix opinion was observed for this aspect and it was observed that 41.00 per cent of the farmers realized its use for agricultural marketing while 35.00 per cent partially realized it and nearly one fourth (24.00 per cent) of them did not realize this feature of internet.

The results point out that majority (69.00 per cent) of the respondents agreed with the statement that "Internet can be a very useful mean to the farmers during present time". It was exciting to note that majority (61.00) percent of the farmers did not believe that use of internet is only time pass activity. It means that they opined it as a useful medium for farming community. Of course, farmers are not in position to use this information for the development of their agriculture because whatever sites available on agriculture are in English language. This fact was reflected in study so 88.00 percent of the farmers partially or absolutely realized that information available on Internet is difficult to understand.

It was really pleasing to note that majority (86.00 percent) of the farmers out of them 56.00 per cent totally and 30.00 per cent partly assumed that development of Indian farmers is possible through Internet. Internet is best mean to learn all now things for young generation, thus, 82.00 percent of the farmers were wishing their children to make positive use of internet at the same time 81.00 per cent of them had opinion that farmers should make use of internet.

The perusal of the data in table 14 revealed that out of the 10 independent variables, five variables like Education, Land holding, Contact with NRI's, Experience of internet use and Mass media exposure were observed positively significant while, remaining five variables such as type of the family was observed negatively significant with the opinion of the farmers about the use of Internet for farming community. The independent variables like Age, Occupation, Animal wealth, Modern agricultural equipment, Type of family, Extension contact and Organization participation were observed non significant with the opinion of the farmers about the use of Internet for farming community.

Summary

Cent per cent respondent was expected the Community Internet Centre (CIC) facilities at village level. Slightly less than cent per cent of them preferred panchayat office as the best place of CIC and they were expecting agriculture graduate with computer knowledge as operator or guide at CIC. The respondents expressed that there should be more than six sets of computer, further they expect that Government should bear expenses to run CIC. The information on farmers' related sites was expected by most of the farmers in Gujarati language that too in the audio-visual form. The major purposes to have CIC explained by the respondents were to collect agricultural information, to collect information on government's programmes, to speedup communication, to exchange information, and to know more about market prices. Majority of the respondents expressed their desire to use Internet daily or twice in a week by their own .All the respondents expressed positive response to have proper training about the use of Internet facility through government agency, at CIC for sustainable agricultural development.

It can be concluded from the results that out of the 10 independent variables, five variables like Education, Land holding, Contact with NRI's, Experience of internet use and Mass media exposure are significantly and positively correlated with the opinion of the farmers about the use of Internet for farming community. More than 70 per cent of the farmers opined that internet is the rich source and fastest way of exchanging information in short time. It must be use by the farming community for their betterment.

Table 1. The expectation of CIC at village level

n = 100

Sr. No	*Type of Expectation*	*Number*	*Per cent*
1	Yes	100	100.00
2	No	00	00.00
	Total	100	100.00

Table 2. Respondent according to choice of the place of CIC

n = 100

Sr. No	*Place*	*Number*	*Per cent*
1	Panchayat	95	95.00
2	Primary school	81	81.00
3	Co-operative Dairy	76	76.00
4	High school	05	05.00
5	Community hall	03	03.00

Table 3. The respondents according to expectation of service

n = 100

Sr. No	*Expectation of service*	*Number*	*Per cent*
1	Operator/Person to Guide and help	98	98.00
2	Printer	72	72.00
3	Separate cabin	68	68.00
4	Collected information in printed form	63	63.00
5	Extra seating facilities	53	53.00

Table 4. Respondents according to choice of person to manage CIC

n = 100

Sr. No	*Person*	*Number*	*Per cent*
1	Agriculture graduate with computer knowledge	98	98.00
2	Educated person of village	76	76.00
3	Expert of computer	57	57.00
4	Primary school teacher	28	28.00

Table 5. Respondents according to their expectation of provision of financial facility

n = 100

Sr. No	*Institution*	*Number*	*Rank*
1	Government	2.00	I
2	Co-operative societies	0.92	III
3	By villagers' sharing	0.07	V
4	Voluntary Donation	0.65	IV
5	Foreign relatives	1.45	II

Table 6. The respondents as per the choice to bear expenses to run CIC

n = 100

Sr. No.	*Responsible for expenditure*	*Number*	*Rank*
1	Government	1.60	I
2	Village Panchayat	1.02	II
3	Co-operative Dairy	0.92	III
4	By collecting charges from users	0.79	IV

Table 7. The Respondents' choice to have minimum computer sets at CIC

n = 100

Sr. No.	*Internet set*	*Number*	*Per cent*
1	1 to 2	00	0.00
2	3 to 4	00	00.00
3	5 to 6	22	22.00
4	More than 6	78	78.00
	Total	**100**	**100.00**

Table 8. Respondents choice on form of information on internet and ICT

n = 100

Sr. No	*Type of information*	*Mean value*	*Rank*
1	In Gujarati language	1.98	I
2	Photographs with written form	1.94	II
3	Audio-visual form	1.91	III
4	Written information	1.42	IV
5	Audio form	1.20	V

Table 9. Respondents according to their purposes to have CIC

n = 100

Sr. No	*Purpose*	*Mean value*	*Rank*
1	To collect agricultural information	1.71	I
2	To collect information on Government's Programmes	1.64	II
3	For speedy communication	1.61	III
4	For exchange information	1.21	IV
5	For entertainment	1.11	V

Sr. No	Purpose	Mean value	Rank
6	To collect information for their children's education	0.74	VI
7	To contact foreign relatives	0.67	VII
8	To contact relatives in India	0.64	VIII
9	To know information on agriculture of developed county	0.56	IX
10	To know more about market prices	0.51	X

Table 10. Respondents' wish to involve in the process of exploring internet

n = 100

Sr. No	Way of internet use	Number	Per cent
1	By own	78	78.00
2	With the help of others	22	22.00
	Total	**100**	**100**

Table 11. Respondents expected frequency to use internet at CIC

n = 100

Sr. No	Expected frequency to use ICT	Number	Per cent
1	Daily	32	32.00
2	Twice in a week	31	31.00
2	Once in a week	06	6.00
3	Once on fortnight	03	3.00
4	Once in month	00	00.00
5	Whenever needed	28	28.00
	Total	**100**	**100.00**

Table 12. Respondents expected agency to receive training to use CIC

n = 100

Sr. No	*Agency*	*Number*	*Per cent*
1	Government	70	70.00
2	Co-operative society	04	04.00
3	NGOs	02	02.00
4	Gram Panchayat	11	11.00
5	Agricultural University	13	13.00
	Total	**100**	**100.00**

Table 13. Opinion of the respondents about use of internet facility

n = 100

Sr. No.	*Statements*	*Opinion*		
		Agree Per cent	*Partially agree*	*Disagree Per cent*
1	Internet can be a very useful mean to the farmers during present time	69.00	10.00	21.00
2	Internet is rich source to collect worldwide information on agriculture and allied fields	71.00	12.00	17.00
3	Internet is fastest way to exchange information in shortest time	72.00	14.00	14.00
4	Internet is costly affair for the farmers	41.00	24.00	35.00
5	Internet is best mean to collect information on market prizes of agricultural product	41.00	35.00	24.00

Sr. No.	Statements	Opinion		
		Agree Per cent	*Partially agree*	*Disagree Per cent*
6	The use of Internet is nothing other than time pass activity	28.00	21.00	61.00
7	Information available on Internet is easy to understand	12.00	41.00	47.00
8	Development of Indian farmers is possible through internet	56.00	30.00	14.00
9	I wish that my children should make positive use of internet facility	81.00	10.00	09.00
10	I wish that farmers should make use of internet	81.00	19.00	00.00

Table 14. Relationship between profile of the farmers and their opinion about internet

No	Independent variables	Correlation coefficient("r" value)
I Personal variable		
1	Age	0.1368
2	Education	0.3263*
II Economic variable		
3	Occupation	-0.0092
4	Land holding	0.2459*
5	Animal wealth	0.0195
6	Modern agricultural equipment	-0.0087

No	Independent variables	Correlation coefficient("r" value)
III Social and communication		
7	Type of family	-0.2472*
8	Contact with NRI's	0.2603*
9	Experience of internet use	0.2718*
10	Mass media exposure	0.2462*
11	Extension contact	0.1239
12	Organization participation	0.1247

* *Significant at 0.05 level of probability*

Reference

Aditya, V. P. S. (2003). ICT for knowledge sharing and enabling supply chain for green produce and products, Paper presented at the National Workshop on "ICT for Agriculture and Rural Development" organized by Indian Association for Information Technology in Agriculture and Dihrubhai Ambani Institute for Information and Communication Technology (DA-IICT), Gandhinagar (Gujarat), India on 18th December 2003.

Buddhadev, B. V. (2003). Crop Production Information System for farmers, Paper presented at the National Workshop on "ICT for Agriculture and Rural Development" organized by Indian Association for Information Technology in Agriculture and

Dihrubhai Ambani Institute for Information and Communication Technology (DA-IICT), Gandhinagar (Gujarat), India on 18th December 2003.

Chauhan,N.M. and Thakor, R.F. (2004). Expectations of the farmers towards Community Internet Centers at Village level. Gujarat Journal of Extension Education **(GJEE)**, Volume-XV December-2004.pp-55-59.

Chauhan, N. M. and Chauhan, N.B. (2006). Farmer's Opinion about use of Internet Technology in Agriculture at village level. Paper presented in National Seminar on Information & Communication Technology: Opportunities and Challenges for Revitalizing Extension System, **December 27-29, 2006** at Navsari Agricultural University, Navsari, Gujarat, held by **Indian Society of Extension Education**.

Mehta, P. (2003). Information Technology in Agriculture: Reaching the un reached, Theme paper presented by at national workshop on ICT for Agriculture and Rural Development organized by Indian Association for Information Technology in Agriculture and Dhirubhai Ambani institute for information an communication technology.

Impact of Organized Retailing on Unorganized Sector

INTRODUCTION

Retailing is one of the pillars of the Indian economy and accounts for 35% of GDP. Retailing in India came with evolutionary patterns from Kirana store to Super market. This sector was un-organized in the initial stage, and after that it carried forward and Now it is growing as supermarket and hypermarket. The paper will depict the main drivers of the retail revolution in India and how this revolution changes the buying behaviour of the customer, increase in disposable income of middle class, infrastructure development and changing customer choice. Organized Retailing is introduced in the last decade and has emerged as one of the sunrise industries in India. The paper will mention the impact of organised retailing on unorganised sector. The study will indicate how the consumers will be benefited form organised retailers. The survey will be carried for limited number of organised retail outlets in Delhi / NCR only and on the basis of that result findings will be mentioned. Based on the results of the surveys, the study will made a number of specific policy recommendations for regulating the interaction of large retailers with small suppliers and for strengthening the competitive response of the unorganized retailers. The survey intends to analyse the consumer behaviour towards organised and unorganised retailing in India, their source of purchasing and the factors which influence their mall purchasing in India. Lastly the paper will mention the current scenario of retail sector in India.

Retail. "Retail" originates from a French word retailer, which means to cut a piece off or to break bulk. Retailer is someone who cuts off or sheds a small piece from something. Retailing is the set of activities that markets products or services to final consumers for their own personal or household use. It does this by organizing their availability on a relatively large scale and supplying them to customers on a relatively small scale. Retailer is a Person or Agent or Agency or Company or Organization who is instrumental in reaching the Goods or Merchandise or Services to the End User or Ultimate Consumer.

Retailing. Retailing is buying in large quantity from a whole seller or directly from a manufacturer and selling the goods/ services to consumer for personal consumption. Retailing is defined as a conclusive set of activities or steps used to sell products or services to consumers. Retailing consists of the business activities involved in selling goods and services to consumers for their personal, family and household use. It includes every sale of goods and services to the final consumers. Retailing is the last stage in the distribution process. In contrast wholesaling is an intermediate stage in the distribution process during which goods and services are not sold to the final consumers but to the business customers.

The retail industry in India has undergone a rapid growth in the organised sector since the year 2000. The volume of total retail sales in India during the year 2004-05 is estimated at Rs. 7, 50,000 and the market is expected to grow at the rate of 2.5% per annum. During this period the retail sector accounted for 10% of the GDP in India. The organised retail sales volume in 2004-05 had just about 2% share of the total retail sale. In present competitive scenario its very important to compete with the competitors and sustain ahead, all companies are analyzing and doing research to know and understand the consumer buying behaviour for the same. According to one Press Release on KPMG Report dated 28 September, 2005, The organized retail sector is expected to grow stronger than GDP growth in the next five years driven by changing lifestyles, strong income growth and favourable demographic patterns. The structure of retailing is developing rapidly with shopping malls becoming increasingly common in large cities, and development plans being projected at 150 new shopping malls by 2008. According to the report, the annual growth of department stores has been estimated at 24%, which is faster than overall retail; and supermarkets have taken an increased share of general food and grocery trade over the last two decades. According to AT Kearney's seventh annual Global Retail Development Index (GRDI), India ranked 5th largest retail destination globally in 2008. The share of retail trade in the country's gross domestic product (GDP) was between 8–10% in 2007. It is currently around 12%, and is likely to reach 22% by 2010.

Objectives. This survey intends to analyse the impact of organised retailing on unorganised retail sector in Delhi/NCR. This research explicates various aspects like the perceived and expected levels of satisfaction of the consumers and the factors which unorganised retailer should take cognizance of in the course of establishing and enhancing their business. The objectives of the research are:

- To find out the consumer behaviour towards organised (supermarkets/malls, hypermarkets, departmental stores etc) and unorganised (local kirana stores, weekly bazaars etc) retail stores in Delhi/NCR.
- To find out the consumers satisfaction level from organised retail stores as well as unorganised retail stores.

The conclusions and the results drawn from this project will go a long way in helping the unorganised retailers in identifying the benefits, which the customers expect from them. However the research will help organised and unorganised retailers in attracting the customers keeping in mind their demands.

Methodology. The survey is based on interviewing grocery store consumers at various catchment areas in Delhi/NCR. Four areas Ghaziabad, Indrapuram, Kaushambi, Laxmi Nagar are selected based on number of households and income groups in the catchments. The data is collected using a random sample of consumers. Consumers who have significant knowledge of the topic were identified and selected at random for questioning. As per questionnaire, interviews were conducted face to face so as to capture the attitude and experience of consumers who had just purchased grocery items from organised and unorganised retail outlets. Both qualitative and quantitative data analysis is done in order to get deeper insights into the consumer behaviour and store loyalty for local grocery stores. Larger the sample size greater is the precision or reliability when research is replicated. But constraints on time, manpower and costs have influenced decisions on the study sample size.

Indian Retail Industry

The Indian retail market is the fifth largest retail destination globally. The current size of the Indian retail industry stands at $511 billion in 2008. Simultaneously, modern retail is likely to increase its share in the total retail market to 22% by 2010. Organised retail in India ranked in US$ 25.44 billion turnover in 2007-08 as against US$ 16.99 billion in 2006-07, a whopping growth rate of 49.73% (according to the Credit Rating and Information Services of India). Organised retail has increased its share from 5% of total retail sales in 2006 to 8% in 2007. India has one of the largest numbers of retail outlets in the world. Of the 12 million retail outlets present in the country, nearly 5 million sell food and related products. Though the market has been dominated by unorganised players, the entry of domestic and international organised players is set to change the scenario. Per capita retailing space is about 2 sq. ft. India's per capita retailing space is thus the lowest in the world. Around 7% of the population in India is engaged in retailing[1]. In India the retail sector is divided in two broad sectors Unorganised Retailing and Organised Retailing.

1. Report named as "Trends on Retail Trade" Compiled by Economic Cell AEPC, available at http://aepc.fibre2fashion.com/vol1issue50/

Unorganised Retailing

Unorganised Retailing, refers to the traditional formats of low-cost retailing, for example, the local *kirana* shops, owner manned general stores, *paan/beedi* shops, convenience stores, hand cart and pavement vendors, etc. Retail sector in India is having one of the highest density of retail outlets per capita in the world and lowest per capita retail space. Indian retail is dominated by a large number of small retailers consisting of the local *kirana* shops, owner-manned general stores, chemists, footwear shops, apparel shops, *paan and beedi* shops, hand-cart hawkers, pavement vendors, etc. which together make up the so-called "unorganized retail" or traditional retail.

Organised Retailing

Organised Retailing refers to trading activities undertaken by licensed retailers, that is, those who are registered for sales tax, income tax, etc. These include the corporate-backed hypermarkets and retail chains, and also the privately owned large retail businesses.

Impact of Organised Retailing on Unorganised Sector

Unorganized retailers in the vicinity of organized retailers experienced a decline in their volume of business and profit in the initial years after the entry of large organized retailers. According to the Indian Council for Research in International Economic Relations (ICRIER), there would be no long term impact due to the entry of organised retail chains on the neighbourhood *kirana* shops in the country. In clear terms the impact of organised retailing on unorganised sector is as follows:

1. The adverse impact on sales and profit weakens over time.
2. There is some decline in employment in the North and West regions which, however, also weakens over time.
3. The rate of closure of unorganized retail shops in gross terms is found to be 4.2% per annum which is much lower than the international rate of closure of small businesses
4. The rate of closure on account of competition from organized retail is lower still at 1.7% per annum.

The Kirana stores and pan shops are seen as part of community life and hence unorganised retail will stay but ICRIER observes that if organised retail does not grow, the unorganised sector will not be able to handle the surging demand. Hence the share of organised retail will grow at a rate between 45 and 50% per annum. The observation rings true as well, this is being witnessed in some urban centres already.

It has come out with certain valuable recommendations. It suggests a nationwide uniform licensing policy to aid modern retailing which will help carry the countries retail sector to the USD (US Dollar) 590 billion mark in 2011-12. It suggests better access to cheaper institutional credit so the Kirana stores can take on competition from organised retail. Presently, only 12% of unorganised retail enjoys access to institutional credit. Another recommendation by ICRIER is worth a serious try. It suggests cash and carry outlets which will sell to unorganised retail and procure from farmers. This can help unorganised retail to buy at wholesale prices for eventual retailing, thereby generating a handsome margin. Farmers too can benefit since they can sell at lucrative prices and realise the sale proceeds in a swift and transparent manner. Once this cushion is provided, unorganised retail can have no grouse against the government and even if it has, the government can ignore it.

Being unorganised retailing is at serious step; there are still challenges for organised retailing in India. Traditional retailing has been established in India for some centuries. It has a low cost structure, mostly owner operated, has negligible real estate and labour costs and little or no taxes to pay. Consumer's familiarity that runs from generation to generation is one big advantage for the traditional retailing sector. In contrast, players in the organised sector have big expenses to meet, and yet have to keep prices low enough to be able to compete with the traditional sector. Moreover, organised retailing also has to cope with the middle class psychology that the bigger and brighter sales outlet is, the more expensive it will be.

Key Drivers of Retailing in India

1. **Consumer Pull.** Over the last decade there has been a significant evolution in the Indian consumers, mainly due to the Liberalization of the consumer goods industry that was initiated in the mid-eighties and accelerated through the nineties, combined with a growing consumerism driven by the media, new opportunities and increasing wealth. Although this change is most noticeable in the metros, it has affected consumers in small towns as well. Consumers can be divided into two broad segments:

   (i) ***High – Income Segment.*** This comprises consumers who do not shop themselves, have a very low level of involvement and whose monthly grocery bill form s a very small part of the salary.

(ii) ***Middle and Lower Income Group.*** This includes consumers who are highly involved in grocery shopping, as this expenditure constitutes 50% or more of the monthly salary. This segment is highly value-conscious, constantly looking for bargains and is made up of active shoppers. Modern retailing characterised by value, variety, convenience and service for the consumers, appeals to this second segment. Supermarkets allow consumers to interact more directly with the products, read labels, compare prices, avail of promotions and offers and so on.

2. **Rising Incomes:** over the past decade, India's middle and high-income population has grown at a rapid pace of over 10% per annum. Though this growth is most evident in urban areas, it has also taken place in rural markets. Further, the number of households earning above Rs. 1, 50,000 per annum is about 80million today and is expected to grow to 200 million by 2015. This growing high-income population is triggering the demand for consumer goods, leading to the proliferation of higher quality/higher priced products. The chart shows the growth of Income and consumption with their respective years[2].

---

2. Dutta Devangshu "The Indian Retail Market", chapter 1. available at http://thirdeyesight.in/articles/India_Retail_Report_2009_chapter-1_Third_Eyesight.pdf

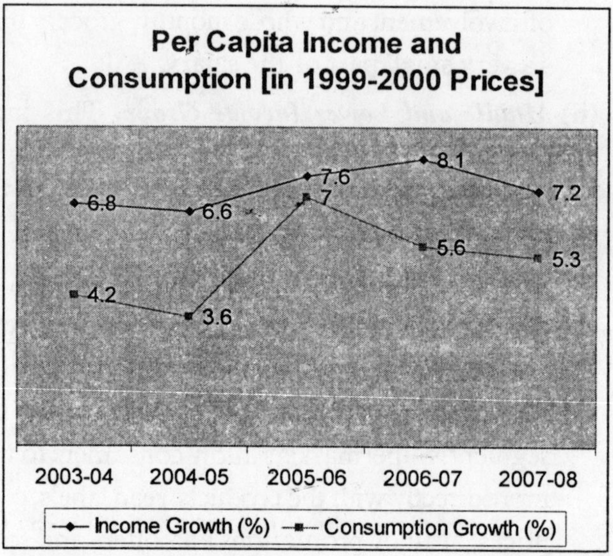

3. **Explosion of media.** There has been an explosion in media as well during the past decade. Kick-started by the cable explosion during the Gulf War, television has accelerated to a point where there are more cable connections than telephones in Indian homes and about 70 channels are being aired at all times. This media bombardment has exposed the Indian consumers to the lifestyles of more affluent countries and raised their aspiration and expectations from the shopping experience. With this Indian consumers want more choice, value, services, experience and convenience.

4. **Change in Consumer behaviour.** The urban woman is literate and in many cases employed. There is greater work pressure and increased commuting time. And with a swift in a family structure, nuclear families have become a significant component of urban markets.

According to a market research conducted in Bangalore, the share of nuclear families is estimated to be as high as 70%. Besides all these factors, the increase in the variety, quality and availability of products, and higher spending power has led to the growing popularity of supermarkets. There has been a change in shopping behaviour in urban India over the past few years with consumers looking for convenience. That is, they want everything under one roof and a bigger choice of products. With an increase in double-income households, people do not have much leisure time and seek the convenience of one-stop shopping in order to make the best use of their time. They also look for speed and efficiency. Increased awareness has also meant that consumers now seek for information, variety, product availability, better quality and hygiene as well as increased customer service. The concept of "Value for Money" is picking up.

5. **Consumerism Cycle.** The consumer cycle starts with the industry dictating the market. Eventually overtime the distributor gains control over the market; at this stage the distributor becomes an important link between manufacturer and customer. When the market starts developing and expanding its horizons, retailers turn into the vital link in the supply chain. India is entering the third stage where retailers control the market. Being the closest link to the consumer in the supply chain, retailers benefit accordingly. Manufacturers spend a lot of money promoting a product, but if it's not on the shop shelf, consumers won't be able to buy it. Manufacturers have

also realized that retailer recommendations matter, particularly in smaller towns where retailers are figures of authority or opinion leaders. With shopping attitudes changing, the Indian market today desires value-added products and services with good ambience and brands, which only a retailer can provide. Hence good retailer relations are a must. Manufacturers are ready to pay listing fees to get retailers to stock a product, or display charges to place it prominently.

6. **The Rural Marketing-Waking Up.** The rural market is beginning to emerge as an important consumption area, accounting for over one-third of the demand for most key consumer durables and non-durable products. In response, manufactures of consumer goods – both FMCGs and durables – have begum developing new products (LG Television, shampoo sachets, Ruf n Tuf jeans) and marketing strategies (using a village "haat" for brand promotions) with the rural consumer in mind.
7. **Establishment of the Supply Chain.** over the past few years, the consumer goods sector has been transformed by increased liberalization, continuous reduction in custom duty, a shift from quota to tariff-based systems for imports and sophistication in manufacturing. Entry restrictions for multinationals have been removed in nearly all sectors. All this has enabled chain retailers to enjoy better range depth and sourcing options as well as improved average margins. There has been a proliferation in the range across al categories, with a simultaneous increase in the supply of products and quality retail space. According to a study, there are over

18,000 stock-keeping units (SKUs are products and their variants, of type and size, counted individually), while most retailers have the space for at most 5,000-7,000 units. This has tempted a number of real estate companies and other corporate into investing in malls and other retail formats.

8. **Entry of the Corporate Sector.** In contrast to the situation only about a decade ago, the level of interest in retailing as a growth opportunity has increased visibly now. Many organisations in India that have been so long dealing directly with the primary distributional channel to reach customers have today embarked on teaching customer first hand by means of retailing by themselves. ITC as we are aware has taken to retailing as a serious business propositions and as a strategic move. Corporate giants in India like Bharti, Reliance and A.V. Birla have embarked on their retail initiatives. A few others like Tatas and Raheja's who are already into retailing are fast diversifying into retailing are fast diversifying into retailing new categories like food. The TATA group has tied up with Woolworth for supporting its croma venture. The future group is on an expansion spree, yet innovating various formats of retailing while trying to offer everything for everyone everywhere in India. The retail advancement is amazing as corporate giants are currently spearheading the retail growth in India.

9. **Expansion of Family Owned Business.** The most successful of these are the Rs. 450 crore Viveks, the 40 year old Chennai consumer durables chain, the Rs. 3,558 crore Pantaloons Apparel retail businesses, and

Bangalore's food Retailer Nilgiris. With the new age demanding consumer preferring to shop in this big retail chains, traditional 'bania' shops will face a difficult time trying to meet consumer expectations. This will make retailing an unattractive proposition for them. The process is likely to be kick-started by grocery stores transforming into supermarkets since the margins in the grocery trade are the lowest in the business.

10. **Building Chains around Brands.** Apparel, footwear and consumer durable brands have driven the growth of speciality chains and upgraded existing multi-brand outlets. Some like Reebok claim to have entered retailing because of the paucity of suitable multi-brand retailing options. However, many of these are emerging as large retailers (Titan, Madhura Garments, Raymonds) today, and appear to be committed to developing their retail businesses. Thus there is an extension of consumer brand-seeking (promise, trust, comfort, image) from products to stores.
11. **Foreign Retailers looking for Entry Options.** the increasing attractiveness of the sector has drawn the interest of global retailers. With the opening up of the economy, more and more MNCs have entered the Indian Business arena through joint ventures, franchisees or even self owned stores. The very first MNC to get into the business was Spencer's, a tie up between the RPG Group and Dairy Farm International; a $10 billion Hong Kong based company, and a part of the Jardine Matheson group. While foreign retailers cannot start operations on their own mainly because of FDI

restrictions on the sector, a number of companies, including Wal-Mart, Tesco, Kingfisher, Metro, Carrefour and Ahold, are exploring entry options. In apparel, Bentton, Lifestyle and Zegno are already in business and Dairy Farm has a number of retailing joint ventures in India.

12. **Technological Impact.** Technology is probably the most dynamic change agent in the retailing industry. The computerization of the various operations in a retail store – including inventory management, billing and payments as well as database management – widespread use of Bar Coding, Point-of-Sale terminals and Management Information System (MIS) has changes the face of retailing drastically. Apart from providing the retailers with better and timely information about their operations, the technology also performs such tasks as preventing threat, promoting the stores goods and creating a better shopping atmosphere. This is done with the help of closed-circuit televisions, video walls, in-store video networks, and other forms of interactive applications – ranging from CD-ROMs to virtually reality – to let customers select and buy products. They make a customers life much easier by facilitating the use of credit cards, debit cards and smart cards. Toll – free numbers have brought about a revolution in consumer ordering and feedback mechanisms. These also pave the way for tele-shopping and net-shopping. Emerging technologies also facilitate just-in-time management of certain products within the store.

Analysis of Customer's behaviour

Consumer behaviour in retailing is more unpredictable & volatile than ever before and retailers are striving to develop new effective strategies for satisfying needs and wants of consumers. Consumers are demanding a very large selection of producers with deep discounts. They are no longer as influenced by brand names but very cautious about quality & value. Thus the retailers focusing on providing best price serve and selection in the form of value will be successful.

1. 34% customers prefers unorganised retail shopping while 26% customers prefers organised retail shopping but 40% customers are still in dilemma.

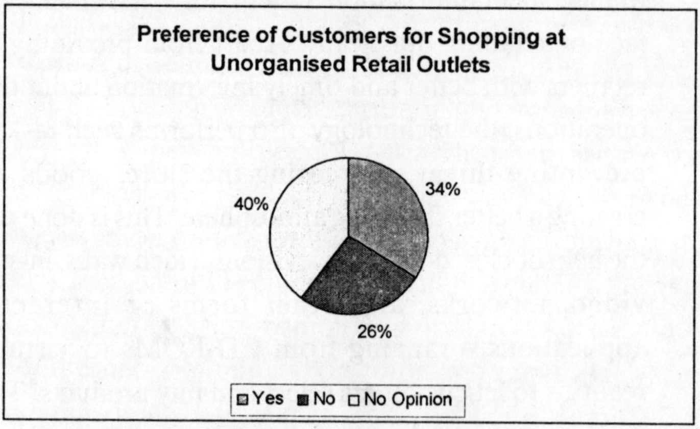

2. 37% customer's purchases daily groceries from local kirana stores while 26% customers shop from Supermarkets, 21% customers from Convenience Stores and rest 16% Customers prefer Hypermarket. Thus, highest percentage is still with local kirana stores

however the difference between supermarket and local kirana is less.

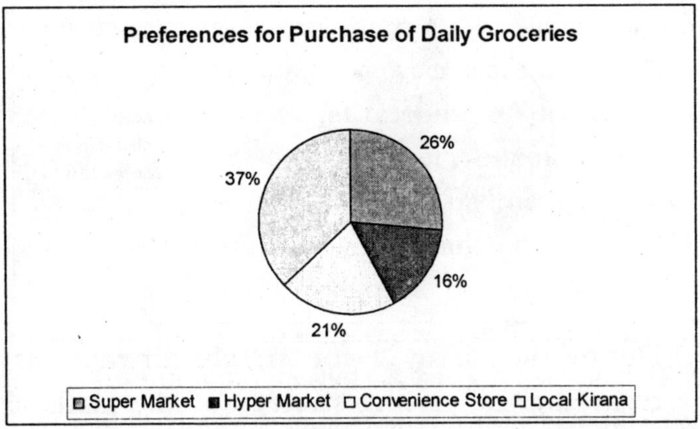

3. 40% Customers visit fortnightly to the malls for various different purposes, 30% customers visit weekly, 20% monthly and rest 10% Daily.

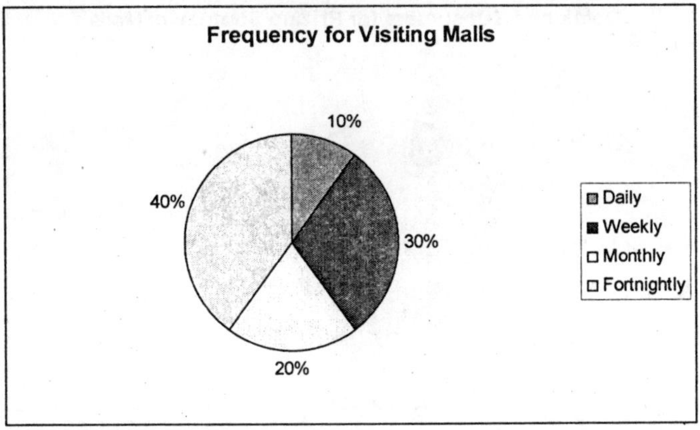

4. 36% Customers visit mall for Shopping, while 38% visits for Entertainment and rest 16% visits for Window shopping.

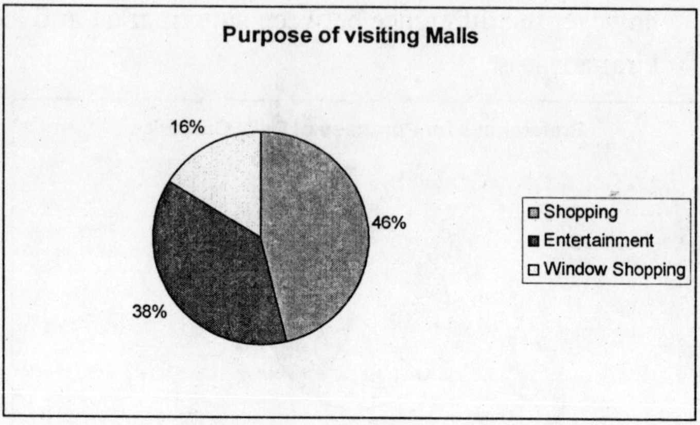

5. During the survey, I got straight forward answer regarding the pricing strategy of the malls. 60% Customers are satisfied with the pricing strategy of the malls after considering various discounts, sales and other offers, while 40% Customers are not satisfied.

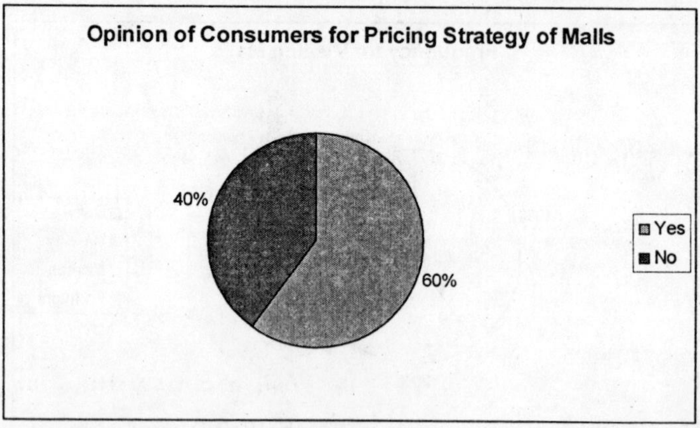

6. During the survey, it was found 64% consumers finds best shopping deals in malls with various Discount offers, gift packages etc. 28% customers are satisfied with the shopping deals served by the local kirana stores while 8% customers has no opinion.

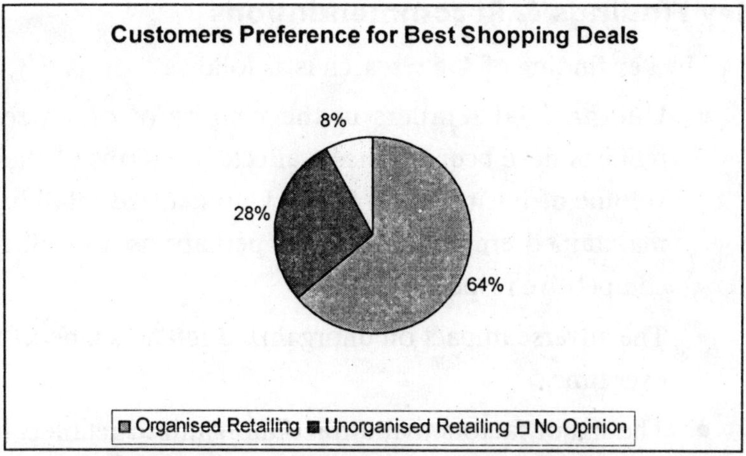

7. 32% of sampled consumers declared an increase in spending, 21% indicated a decrease and the balance no change. Thus the arrival of organized retail has enhanced spending in general. The reasons indicated for higher spending have been mainly the purchase of larger quantities due to wider range of products, availability of attractive offers like discounts and promotional schemes, and access to better quality products with higher price.

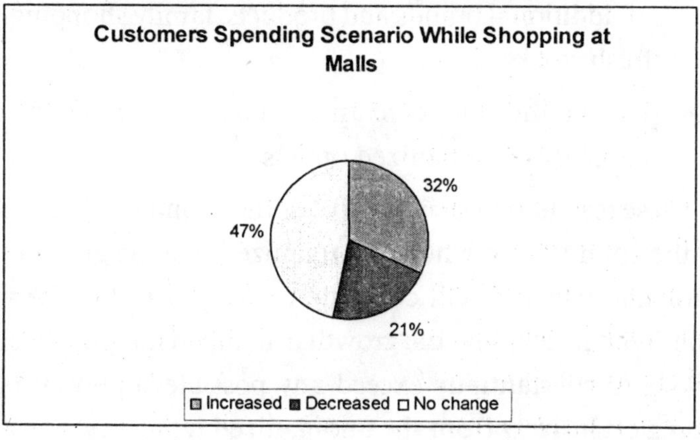

Key Findings & Recommendations

The key finding of the research is as follows:

- Unorganized retailers in the vicinity of organized retailers have been adversely affected in terms of their volume of business and profit. Unorganized retail has maintained employment levels perhaps as a result of competitive response.
- The adverse impact on unorganized retailers tapers off over time.
- The major factors that attract unorganized retailers to consumers are proximity, goodwill, credit sales, bargaining, loose items, convenient timings, and home delivery.
- There is clear evidence of a competitive response from traditional retailers who are gearing up to meet the threat from organized retailers.
- Consumers have generally gained with the emergence of organized outlets through the availability of better quality products, lower prices, one-stop shopping, choice of additional brands and products, family shopping, and fresh stocks.
- Lower income consumers have saved more from purchases at organized outlets.

These results are not indicative of the countrywide scenario. For the country as a whole, unorganized retail is growing at a reasonable rate and will continue to do so for many years to come. Yet it is clear that the growth in demand for retail business is likely to substantially exceed any possible supply response coming exclusively from the unorganized retailers.

India is at the crossroads with regard to the retail sector. Several emerging market economies have gone ahead and reaped the benefits of modern retail. India is however a latecomer to organized retail expansion and the picture still remains unclear as to its future direction. The study advocates a balanced approach to retail and suggests that the government plays a major role in shaping its future course. There is no doubt that traditional retail has been performing a vital function in the economy and is a significant source of employment. However, it suffers from huge inefficiencies as a result of which consumers do not get what they want. In contrast, organized retail provides consumers with a wider choice of products, lower prices, and a pleasant shopping environment. Following are the recommendations:

1. The Government should encourage setting up of modern large cash-and-carry outlets, which could supply not only to *kirana* stores but also to licensed hawkers at wholesale rates.
2. The government should make available credit at reasonable rates from banks and micro-credit institutions for expansion and modernization of traditional retailers.
3. The government should take initiatives to Convert all uncovered wet markets to covered ones and modernize those markets in a time-bound manner with emphasis on hygiene, convenience to shoppers, proper approach roads, entry, exits, etc.
4. Government must facilitate the formation of farmers' co-operatives to directly sell to organized retailers. In this case, while the government could provide tax

incentives and capital subsidies, equity support should be avoided.

Future prospects of Indian Retailing

An Associated Chamber of Commerce and Industry of India (Assocham)-KPMG study has pegged India's total retail market at $353 billion in 2008, which it says is projected to grow at 8% annually to touch $416 billion by 2010. "The organised retail, which currently accounts 7% of the retail market, is projected to grow at a much faster pace of 40% per annum to touch $51 billion by 2010. The unorganised retail sector in India has been the traditional employer to a large number of people across the country. A retail outlet in an unorganised sector feeds a household of six to seven members. The latest edition of India Retail Report, brought out by private research firm Images F and R along with the Confederation of Indian Industry (CII) and other organisations, says the domestic retail market will touch Rs.18.1 trillion (Rs.1,810,000 crore or $402 billion) by 2010.

The past six months have been difficult for the retail industry. Retail has been one of the seven industries in the country that have been severely Impacted by the downturn in economic conditions. The long term prospects for retail chain expansion are still very attractive and this period of uncertainty is seen by retailers as an important consolidation imperative for an industry that has been growing at 30-40% p.a. over the past decade. The relatively low rates of penetration of organized retail in most categories coupled with the sheer Attractiveness of India's demographic and economic environment is expected to continue to add momentum to overall prospects of this Sector in the long term. However with recent developments, some people may feel that the retail boom is over and it may already be too late to enter the Indian market. I beg to differ: I believe there is still a lot of stream, a lot of energy in the Indian market. In fact, it would be most appropriate to quote, "Picture abhi baki hai, mere dost!" ("The movie isn't over yet, my friend!") The road to modernising the retail sector in India is long and we have only taken the first few steps yet. Economically difficult times are wonderful opportunities for shedding flab, challenging existing business models and assumptions, and also provide great frameworks for building efficient and lasting companies. At last I would like to coat Indian Retailing is moving towards a fresh start in 2009!

Summary

The concept of retail is comparatively very old in Indian context. Before any body knew about what retail is, we had kirana stores, medical stores and lot many other stores working surprisingly well all over the country. Recently with the entrance of big players like Walmart or Reliance, people are getting idea of the traditional stores going to be vanished. But just to remind us, we should never forget how deep rooted is this old concept. The very modern organised stores have taken the idea of retailing nowhere else than from these old shops.

The survey concluded that India's organised and unorganised retail sectors can co-exist and flourish. DECISION-MAKING with regard to retail outlet selection is very similar to consumer decision-making on brands where the consumer goes through a process starting from identifying needs to post-purchase issues. The growth in the Indian organized retail market is mainly due to the change in the consumer's behaviour. This change has come in the consumer due to increased income, changing lifestyles, and patterns of demography which are favourable. Now the consumer wants to shop at a place where he can get food, entertainment, and shopping all under one roof. This has given Indian organized retail market a major boost.

While on the other hand the tradition stores are shops where the various product available are the range of product really required by the customers. They cautiously take care of the choice of the customers and bring the product which is demanded by them. They try to satisfy them with the wide range and at the same time maintain a good relationship to retain them and consequently convert them into their loyal customer. These owners also study the emerging trend in the market bring the latest goods to their stores and then learn how is it actually affecting the sales of theirs. Although there stores have comparatively less product range the selection made is quite relevant.

Having looked at the features let us find the loopholes. However good is the ambience and wide is the product range, when it comes the selling price of the various goods, traditional shops are always more efficient than these newly evolved stores. These retail shops lacking the interaction with the customers have miserably failed in building base with loyal customer. No matter how much the companies talk about CRM (customer relationship management), when it comes to the implementation they endeavour it only through the discount sales driven by their profit motive. Thus, in India it is quite sceptical that the organised retail will be ever able to overcome the unorganised retail completely. The values, culture and beliefs of the customers prompt them to go the same retail shop where they can get the product required, at low price and with least waiting time for billing. No matter how lucrative is this sector and how bright is the market; the organised sector in retailing has to go a long way to understand the customer requirement

References

- Joseph Mathew, Nirupama soundararajan, Manisha Gupta, Sanghamitra Sahu "Impact of Organised Retailing on Unorganised Sector"Working paper No. 222, ICRIER, Sep. 2008.
- Retail report by KPMG in India, March, 09, "Consumer Markets Indian Retail: Time to change lanes"
- http://pibmumbai.gov.in/scripts/detail.asp?releaseId=E2008PR1013
- http://www.thehindubusinessline.com/2008/05/27/stories/2008052751470500.htm
- http://www.business-standard.com/india/storypage.php?tp=on&autono=38292
- http://www.merinews.com/catFull.jsp?articleID=134755
- http://www.dnaindia.com/money/report_organised-unorganised-retailers-can-co-exist-in-india_1195909

ICT – Revolutionizes E-commerce and E-Business

INTRODUCTION

In the emerging global economy, E-commerce and E-Business have increasingly become a necessary component of business strategy and a strong catalyst for economic development. The integration of information and communications technology (ICT) in business has revolutionized relationships within organizations and those between and among organizations and individuals. Specifically, the use of ICT in business has enhanced productivity, encouraged greater customer participation, and enabled mass customization, besides reducing costs.

With developments in the Internet and Web-based technologies, distinctions between traditional markets and the global electronic marketplace-such as business capital size are gradually being narrowed down. E-Business is a new business paradigm, a new concept floating around for some years now. It helps connect stakeholders electronically at any time and anywhere around the world. It is a business in cyberspace providing equal opportunity to everybody who has access to Internet Technology. E-Business (electronic business), is the conduct of business on the Internet, not only buying and selling but also servicing customers and collaborating with business partners. It is one of the catalysts for globalised economic activities which have brought enormous wealth to some countries in the developed world. Some developing countries, for example, India is reaping benefit out of the globalization. Rapid technological change is having a profound influence on how we organize and conduct businesses. More significantly, the Internet makes it possible to transform electronic trading from an expensive and specialized process into a cheap and convenient method for all. This paper will depict the investment done by the organization in E-commerce especially in B2B and B2C model. The paper will also highlight the revenues earned by the countries and organizations through E-commerce specially in context with Amazon.com. The secondary data will be used for the research. The paper will elaborate the Impact of recession on E-commerce Investment and revenue generation. The finding and suggestions expected to come up after the research will provide input for further improvements and future Prospects of E-Business.

Until the last few centuries, there were two main Revolutions – the Industrial Revolution and the Electronic Revolution. The Industrial revolution transformed our society from agricultural based to industrial based and the electronic revolution transferred our society from mechanical to electronic based. This 21st Century is the beginning of new revolution, i.e. network revolution. It interconnects the different parts of the world together and the concept of globalisation comes into existence. The internet is the engine of this revolution and E-commerce is the fuel. The idea of conducting business transaction via electronic media is an integral part of many businesses for several decades. But due to the advancement of internet technologies and advanced cryptographic techniques, E-commerce comes into the existence.

Evolution of Commerce: Commerce has evolved over the centuries. Prior to the evolution of money, it was a simple barter process; the evolution of money brought with it the concept of "market place". In market place, commerce is function of 4p's – Product, Price, Place and Promotion. It was realised that with the slightest modification of 2Ps i.e. Price and Place, can bring the convenience to the customer of getting product at their home. With this concept of street vendor was born, afterwards the concept of mail-order cataloguing and tele-shopping came into existence with development of media vehicle

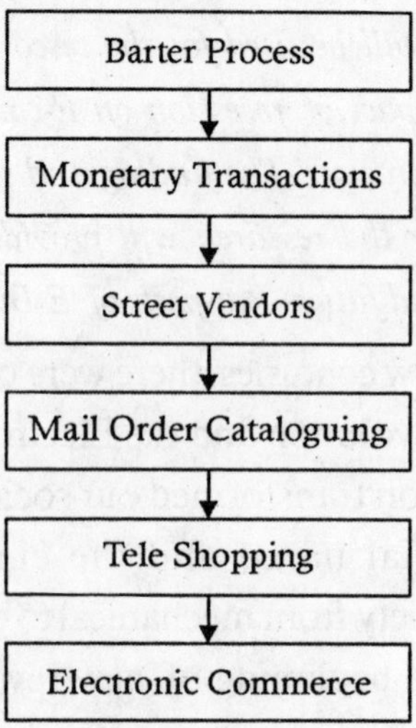

The latest generation of commerce is one that can be done over internet. Internet provides a virtual platform to buyers and sellers to sell and buy the goods and services. The commerce over internet is known as "Electronic commerce" or "E-commerce". E-commerce has emerged as boundary less trade medium in the era of globalisation.

Global recession. A global recession is a period of global economic slowdown. The International Monetary Fund (IMF) takes many factors into account when defining a global recession, it states that global economic growth of 3% or less is "equivalent to a global recession".

Recession. Period of general economic decline, defined usually as a contraction in the GDP for six months (two consecutive quarters) or longer.

Electronic Business. It is commonly referred as "**E-Business**", it may be defined as the utilization of information and communication technologies (ICT) in support of all the activities of business.

Electronic Commerce. Electronic **commerce or E-commerce (E com)** is a subset of E-Business. E-commerce is the purchasing, selling, and exchanging of goods and services over computer networks (such as the Internet) through which transactions or terms of sale are performed electronically.

Types of Ecommerce. Ecommerce can be broken into four main categories:

- **B2B (Business-to-Business).** Companies doing business with each other such as manufacturers selling to distributors and wholesalers selling to retailers. Pricing is based on quantity of order and is often negotiable. Like alibaba.com is B2B website.

- **B2C (Business-to-Consumer).** Businesses selling to the general public typically through catalogs utilizing shopping cart software. Google is the good example of B2C website.
- **C2B (Consumer-to-Business).** A consumer posts his project with a set budget online and within hours companies review the consumer's requirements and bid on the project. The consumer reviews the bids and selects the company that will complete the project. Ebay.com is C2B website.
- **C2C (Consumer-to-Consumer).** where individuals can buy and sell thanks to online payment systems like Paypal where people can send and receive money online with ease.

New Technological Innovation: E-Business

Year 1830-1900 was a time of rapid economic growth and technological innovation which has been well documented and analyzed. Business historians Chandler (1977) and Porter and Livesay (1971) discuss changing patterns of production and distribution over this period.

In 1830, almost all goods were generic. Production processes used relatively simple technology and were low volume, with nearly all products distributed within a small locality. The historical trend identified is the increasingly concentrated nature of the market, and the reduced costs of exchange. Changes in technology and market conditions created an economic situation that favored manufacturer-controlled distribution systems. However, that new technology (E-Business) is an important contributing factor to the changing organizational structure of firms. The four ways in which technological innovations can have impact: by necessitating new organizational structures to handle complexities, by encouraging administrative or other process changes that reduce costs or improve efficiency, by facilitating the development of new distribution channels, and by changing the power relations amongst organizations.

E-Business Worldwide

With over 1.2 billion Internet users worldwide in 2007, E-commerce has seen unprecedented growth over the last decade. Most retailers have taken advantage of this lucrative arena and have created a presence on the Internet, targeting the immense buying power of worldwide online shoppers. In 2009, online spending by consumers online purchases will rise by a substantial 13.3% to £20.9 billion although the internet is undoubtedly starting to slow and become a much more competitive environment, online retail is still set to reach £31.2 billion by 2013, accounting for 10.0% of total retail spending. In 2009, total retail growth will contract by 0.6% as consumer spending is ravaged by the effects of the recession. However, the online market will expand by a substantial 13.3% over the course of the year, driven by the continued increases in the number of internet shoppers and higher expenditure per head. This follows on from the trend of 2008 when there was a 1.0% increase in internet users—to 34.4m—and an 18.1% increase in online shoppers—to 26.7m—with each of these individuals spending an average of 5.8% more in comparison to 2007. Although online growth in 2008 represented a substantial out performance of wider retail, it was also the smallest rise in the channel's sales since the dotcom bubble burst in 2002. There are a growing number of signs that the internet is beginning to mature and enter a new, more subdued phase of growth, Growth in the number of online shoppers in 2008 was strong, but considerably less than the growth seen in 2007. It is predicted that these growth rates will continue to fall over the next five years, as penetration of the population begins to level out.

Korea's total. E-commerce transaction for year 2006-2007 is

Transaction Category	*2006 (US $ thousand)*	*RATE*	*2007 (US $ thousand)*	*RATE*	*COMPARISION 2006 vs 2007 (US $ thousand)*	
E-commerce						
Total	413,584	100%	516,514	100%	102.930	24.9%
B2B	366,191	88.3%	464,456	89.9%	98,264	26.8%
B2C	9,132	2.2%	10,226	2.0%	1,094	2%
C2C	3,826	0.9%	5,032	1.0%	1,206	31.5%

The **world wide E-commerce** transactions are

YEAR	*US$ Billion*
2007	240
2006	190
2005	150
2004	130
2003	100
2002	80
2001	70
2000	50
1999	25
1998	10

The share of B2B in total global E-commerce was 79.2% during 2000 and rose to 87% during 2004. According to the regions B2B E-commerce in $ billions during 2000-04 were as under

Year / Region	*2000*	*2001*	*2002*	*2003*	*2004*	*As % of world wide B2B commerce 2004*
North America	159.2	316.8	563.9	964.3	1600.8	57.7
Asia/ Pacific	36.2	68.6	121.2	199.3	300.6	10.8
Europe	26.2	52.4	132.7	334.1	797.3	28.7
Latin America	2.9	7.9	17.4	33.6	58.4	2.1
Africa/ Middle East	1.7	3.2	5.9	10.6	17.7	0.6
Total	**226.2**	**448.9**	**841.1**	**1541.9**	**2774.8**	**100**

The worldwide sales for B2B category is

YEAR	*B2B Sales(including EDI) US$ Billion*
2007	6800
2006	5300
2005	4100
2004	2800
2003	1600
2002	900
2001	730
2000	600
1999	550
1998	520

The **world wise** E-commerce revenue in percentage in year 2000 and 2004 was

Region	Year 2000	Year 2004
Asia	5%	10%
Western Europe	46%	83%
Rest of the world	7%	7%

E-Business in India

The low cost of the PC and the growing use of the Internet has shown the tremendous growth of Ecommerce in India, in the recent years. According to the Indian Ecommerce Report released by Internet and Mobile Association of India (IAMAI) and IMRB International, "The total online transactions in India was Rs. 7080 crores (approx $1.75 billion) in the year 2006-2007 and grow by 30% to touch 9210 crores (approx $2.15 billion) by the year 2007-2008. Although, as compared to the western countries, India is still in is its initial stage of development. Although business-to-business transactions play an important part in E-commerce market, a share of E-commerce revenues in developed countries is generated from business to consumer transactions. Railway and Airlines have played a vital role in E-commerce transactions in India. Travel portals are exploding in India. Recently MakeMyTrip.com has shown Rs 1000 crores of turnover. Travel alone constituted 50% of Rs 4800 crore online market in 2007-08. In India, online services like ticketing, banking, tax payment, bill payment, hotel room booking, entertainment, online games, matrimonial sites, job sites, etc. are showing signs of development in business-to-customer transactions. There has been tremendous boost in the online E-Business with the stock exchange coming online. Online valentine gifts and Diwali gifts are also becoming popular along with the birthday cakes. No doubt, the total value of the B2B transactions is much larger than that of the B2C transactions, because typically B2B transactions are of much greater value than B2C transactions. It seems that the B2C market in India will take time to grow as compared to the B2B market.

E-Business in the Era of Recession

The economic downturn is leading to the internet playing an increasingly bigger role. The net effect of the recession is likely to make the web a bigger part of retailing because retail chains and consumer goods manufacturers have seen during the recession how consumers use the web to research, even if they buy offline. Actual purchase is not the only aspect of online shopping for customers.

According to the report by Forrester Research and others on E-commerce indicates that E-commerce is one of the very few markets with growth expectations in 2009 and beyond. According to the report E-commerce revenue will grow from $204B to $335B by 2012. It has been believed that online sales will continue to grow through the recession due to accelerating shifts in consumer buyer patterns.

Drop in real U.S. GDP of 1.5% to 1.9% occurs for three to four quarters, it is believed that online retail E-commerce would still increase by 18%. In US the E-commerce rose 14.3% in 2008, but 26.5% overseas. That adds up to 21.5% combined, and even if economic growth slows globally

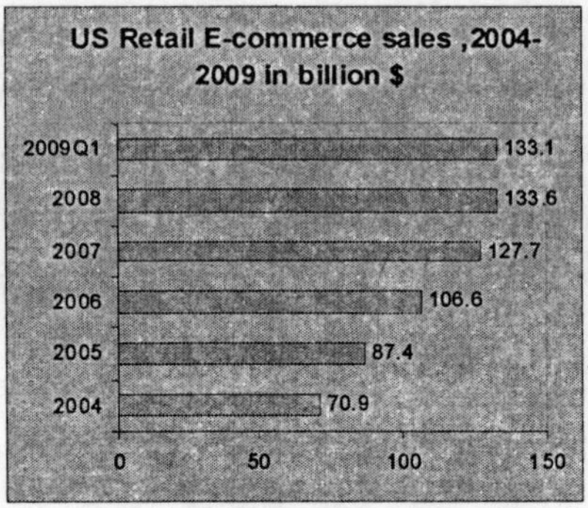

Performance of various B2B and B2C Companies in the Era of Recession

1. Amazon

Company seeks to offer the Earth's Biggest Selection and to be the Earth's most customer- centric company, where customers can find and discover anything they may want to buy online.

Amazon.com, Inc. operates as an online retailer in North America and internationally. It operates various retail Web sites, including amazon.com, amazon.co.uk, amazon.de, amazon.fr, amazon.co.jp, amazon.ca, and amazon.cn. The company serves its consumer customers through its retail Websites and focuses on selection, price, and convenience. It also offers programs that enable seller customers to sell their products on its Websites and their own branded Websites. In addition, the company serves developer customers through Amazon Web Services, which provides access to technology infrastructure that developers can use to enable virtually any type of business. Further, it offers co-branded credit card programs, fulfillment, and other marketing and promotional services, such as online advertising. Amazon.com, Inc. was founded in 1994 and is headquartered in Seattle, Washington.

If Amazon's 66 million active customers all lived in the same country, it would be the world's 19th most populous country, larger than every European country except Germany. And if every US household spent $170 at Amazon.com this year, the total amount they'd spend would still be less than Amazon's 2008 revenues of over $19B. Amazon has used the internet to create a truly global business platform, one which is poised for incredible growth in the coming decade. Sales have surged year over year at the world's largest E-commerce company, with revenues growing 29.1% from 2007 to 2008 due to a combination of low prices, shipping promotions, and rollouts of new product categories.

While most people naturally think of Amazon as the internet superstore that sells products in over forty categories, from books to electronics to groceries to jewellery to auto parts, the company has gradually expanded beyond that simple E-Business platform; today Amazon is simultaneously an E-commerce and internet technology platform, a fulfillment and logistics platform, a search technology, an internet advertising platform, and even an internet start up incubator of sorts.

Recent stock performance

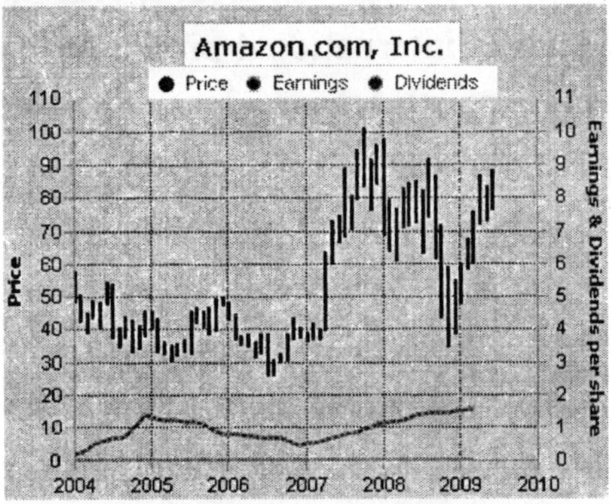

Current Price (7/2/2009): 79.32

(Figures in U.S. Dollars)

Category Expansion

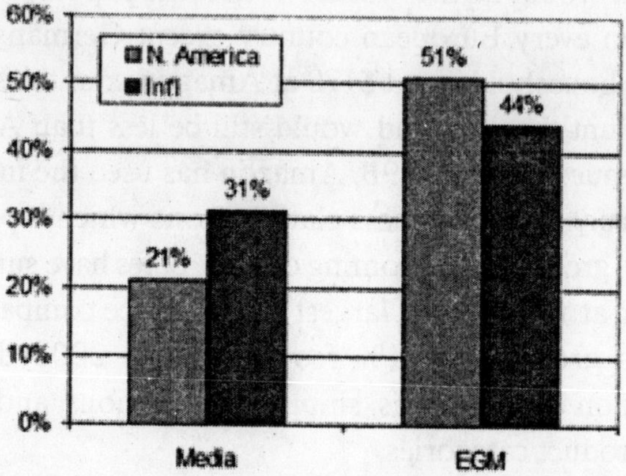

Although 64% of Amazon's worldwide revenue still comes from media categories (books, music, video), Amazon's product footprint in the US has expanded into over 40 categories. New product categories represent significant growth opportunities for the company, given the lower online penetration rates in many of these categories. Revenue and income growth rates for these categories have regularly outpaced the growth in media categories both in the US and abroad. Q3 2007 saw the launch of Apparel & Shoes, Home & Kitchen, and Baby stores for several of Amazon's international presences, and the highly successful Fulfilment by Amazon was expanded to the UK, Germany and Japan as well.

International Expansion

Global Selection

	US	UK	Germany	France	Japan	Canada	China
Books	'95	'98	'98	'00	'00	'02	'04
Music/Video	'98	'99	'99	'00	'01	'02	'04
DVD/Rental*	'98	'99/'04*	'99/'05*	'00	'01	'02	'04
Video Games & Software	'99	'00	'00	'01	'01	'03	'04
Electronics	'99	'01	'01	'05	'03		'04
Toys & Baby	'99	'01	'04	'07	'04		'04
Tools & Hardware	'99	'04	'04				
Kitchen & Housewares	'00	'04	'04		'03		'06
Magazines	'01		'02		'04		
Office Products	'02						
Apparel & Accessories	'02						
Sports & Outdoors	'03	'07	'06		'05		
Gourmet Food	'03						
Jewelry/Watches	'03	'07	'07		'07		'06
Health & Personal Care	'03				'06		'06
Beauty	'04						'06
Musical Instruments	'04						
Grocery	'06						
Automotive	'06						
Third Party Sellers							
Marketplace	'00	'02	'02	'03	'02	'03	
Merchants@	'02	'06	'06		'07		

Expect More Category and Country Expansion Over Time

Business and Financials

Earnings Highlights (Q1 '09):

Amazon.com Inc. released first quarter earnings. Earnings climbed 24 percent to $177 million, or 41 cents per share, compared with $143 million, or 34 cents per share, in the year-ago quarter, to beat the 31 cents per share .

The revenue rose 18 percent to $4.89 billion, slightly higher than analysts' expectations of $4.76 billion. In the first quarter, sales of items such as books, CDs and DVDs rose 7 percent to $2.72 billion, while sales of electronics and other general merchandise rose nearly 39 percent to $2.05 billion.

Amazon Historical Performance

	2006	2007	2008
Net Sales ($millions)	10,711	14,835	19,166
Net Income ($millions)	190	476	645
Operating expenses($millions)	1,966	2,513	3,153
Cash ($millions)	1,022	2,539	2,769
Current Ratio	N/A	1.39	1.30

Revenue/GPM. Amazon.com spent $3.74 billion to make $4.89 billion in revenue. This Gross Profit Margin totaled 23.5%.

Comparison of Growth in Sales between Fiscal Years (2005-2008)

Years	*FY08-FY07*	*FY07-FY06*	*FY06-FY05*
North America (%)	26	38	25
International (%)	33	39	28

This is due in part to the relative maturity of the US market, as well as to the strategy Amazon has employed in rolling out new product categories and features to its international properties. Amazon has typically introduced most of its new stores and features in the US market first, eventually replicating the most successful ventures in international markets. Amazon's international businesses have thus been able to benefit from experience gained through US experiments to grow at an accelerated pace.

REVENUE BY GEOGRAPHY (USD)

PERIOD ENDING	*31-DEC 2004*	*31-DEC 2005*	*31-DEC 2006*	*31-DEC 2007*	*31-DEC 2008*
Revenue - North America	3.85B	4.71B	5.87B	8.10B	10.2B
Revenue - International	3.07B	3.78B	4.84B	6.74B	8.94B
Total Revenue	6.92B	8.49B	10.7B	14.8B	19.2B

REVENUE BY SEGMENT (USD)

PERIOD ENDING	*31-DEC 2004*	*31-DEC 2005*	*31-DEC 2006*	*31-DEC 2007*	*31-DEC 2008*
Revenue - Media	5.10B	5.93B	7.07B	9.24B	11.1B
Revenue - Electronics & Other General Merchandise	1.69B	2.33B	3.36B	5.21B	7.54B
Total Revenue	6.92B	8.49B	10.7B	14.8B	19.2B

2. Google

Google Inc. is an American public Corporation, earning revenue from advertising related to its Internet search, email, online mapping, offline productivity, social networking and video sharing services as well as selling advertising-free versions of the same technologies. The Google headquarters, the googleplex, is located in Mounatain view, California. As of March 31, 2009, the company has 20,164 full-time employees. Google was founded by Larry Page and Sergey Brin while they were students at Stanford University and the company was first incorporated as a privately held company on September 4, 1998. The initial public offering took place on August 19, 2004, raising US$ 1.67 billion, implying a value for the entire corporation of US$23 billion. Google has continued its growth through a series of new product developments, acquisition, partnership, environmentalism; philanthropy and positive employee relation have been important tenets during the growth of Google. Google's mission is "to organize the world's information and make it universally accessible and useful".

The Investment made by the Google during the year 2006, 2007, 2008 and 2009Q1 is as follows

COST	*2006*	*2007*	*2008*	*2009Q1*
Costof revenues	4,225,027	6,649,085	8,621,506	2,101,504
Traffic Acquisition Cost	3,308,777	4,933,878	5,938,951	1,435,960
Other Cost of Revenues	916,250	1,715,207	2,682,555	665,544
Research & Development	1,228,589	2,119,985	2,793,192	641,643
Sales & Marketing	849,518	1,461,266	1,946,244	433,941
General & Administrative	751,787	1,279,250	1,802,639	448,311
Total Costs & Expenses	7,054,921	11,509,586	15,163,581	3,625,399

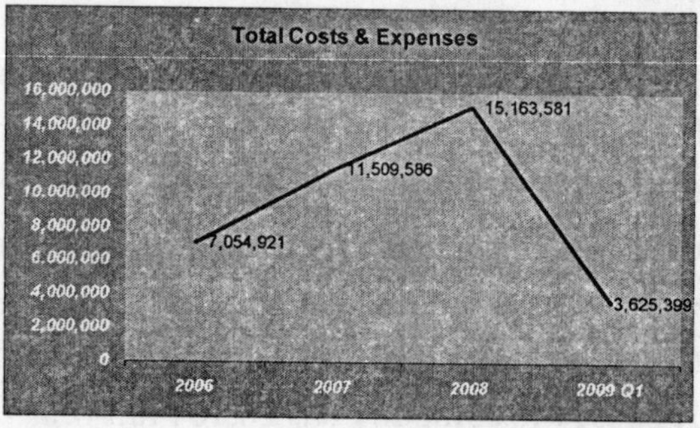

Even during the period of recession Google has invested more than the prior years.

Revenues earned by Google:

Revenues	*2006*	*2007*	*2008*	*2009 Q1*
Revenues	10,604,917	16,593,986	21,795,550	5,508,990
Google web sites	6,332,797	10,624,705	14,413,826	3,692,823
Google Network web sites	4,159,831	5,787,938	6,714,688	1,638,042
Total Advertising Revenues	10,492,628	16,412,643	21,128,514	5,330,865
Licensing & other revenues	112,289	181,343	667,036	178,125

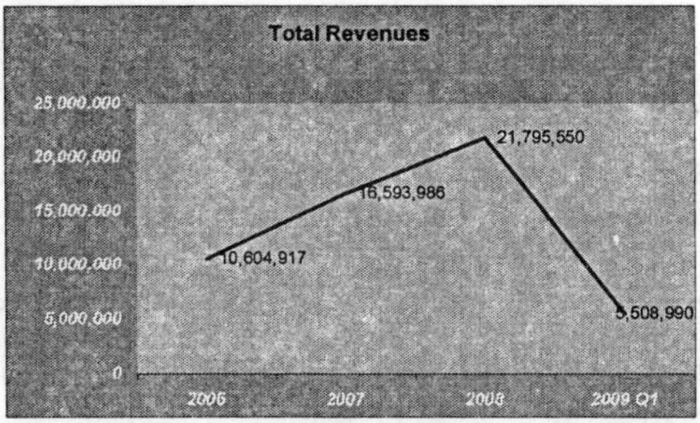

Google has earned good revenues during the period of recession, as the chart indicates the revenue is increasing year by year; there is les effect of recession on B2C companies.

3. Alibaba.com

Alibaba Group is a Hangzhou-based family of Internet-based businesses that include Business-to-business trade, online retail, a payment platform, and business management software and regionalized classified listings. It was founded in 1999 by Ma Yun (Jack Ma), and operates five E-commerce sub-companies which operate different aspects of trading. In 2008, alibaba.com attracted at least 23 million visitors of which 65 percent were from China. Japan's Softbank was one of the earliest investors in Alibaba. Its founder, Masayoshi Son, invested $18 million in the company in 2000 and also participated in subsequent rounds of financing.

As of January 2007, the Alibaba Group is made up of 5 sub-companies:

- **Alibaba.com:** English language global trade website serving small and medium-sized enterprises
- **Taobao.com:** Online auctions web site for customers

- **Alipay:** Online payments web site, processing mainly payments within China
- **Alisoft:** Provider of web services to the Chinese Small and Medium-sized Enterprise marketplace
- **Alimama:** Online advertising exchange, which allows web publishers and advertisers to trade online advertising inventory.

The Revenues earned and the investment made by the Alibaba during the year 2006, 2007, 2008 and 2009Q1 is as follows (in RMB'000)

COST	***2006***	***2007***	***2008 Q1***	***2008 Q4***	***2009Q1***
Cost of Revenue	237,625	280113	78,926	118,252	108,824
Sales and Marketing Expanses	610,198	736,813	201,743	371,286	288,963
Product and development expenses	105,486	131,495	36,592	62,828	60,539
General and Administrative expenses	159,969	229,868	72,210	93,113	83,885
Business Taxes and Surcharge	69,394	110,545	-	-	-
Bandwidth and depreciation expenses	30,983	38,771	-	-	-
Staff cost and other expenses	237,625	280,113	-	-	-

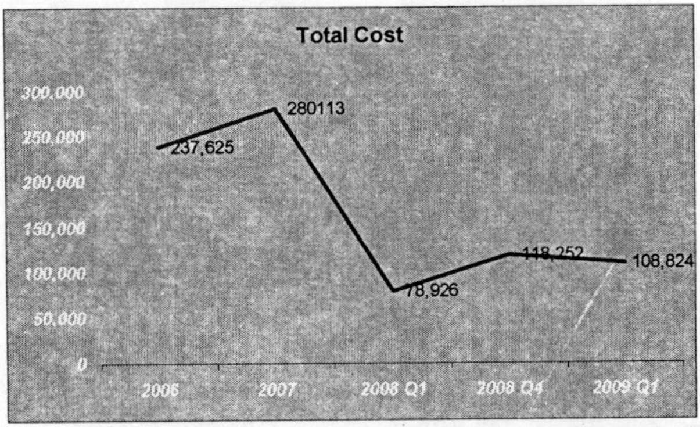

Revenues	*2006*	*2007*	*2008 Q1*	*2008 Q4*	*2009 Q1*
International market place					
Gold Supplier members	967,858	1,503,331	447,630	475,438	492,683
International Trust pass members	24,011	32,825	8,994	12,083	12,876
Other Revenues	-	11,539	7,540	1,583	-
Sub-total	991,869	1,547,695	46,164	489,104	505,559

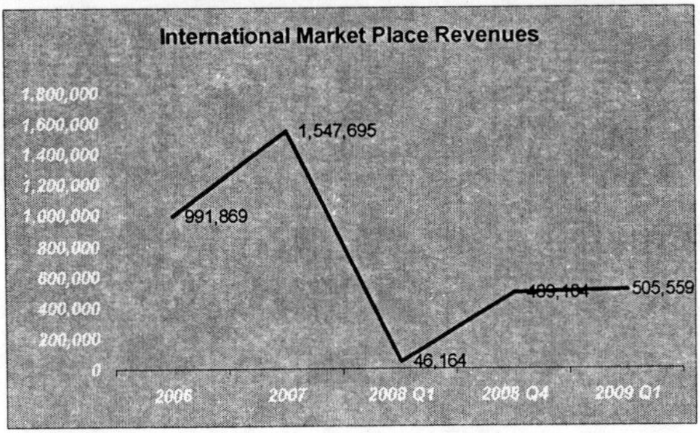

Revenues	*2006*	*2007*	*2008 Q1*	*2008 Q4*	*2009 Q1*
China market place					
China Trust pass members	369,653	594,098	206,127	294,070	288,468
Other Revenues	2,340	20,964	9,790	22,690	12,606
Sub-total	371,993	615,062	215,917	316,760	301,074

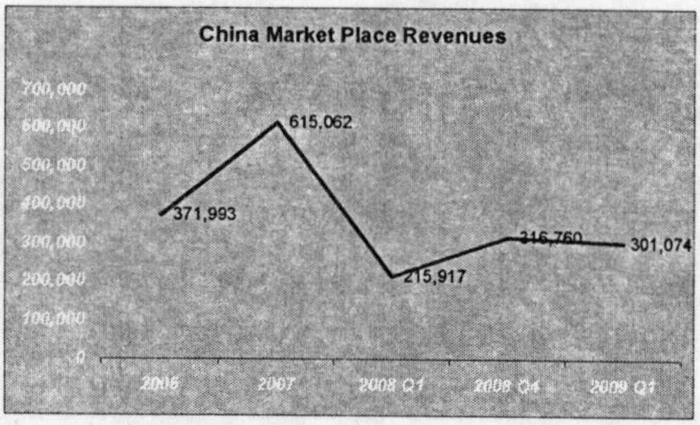

Revenues	2006	2007	2008 Q1	2008 Q4	2009 Q1
Revenues	1,363,862	2,162,757	78,926	118,252	108,824
International market place	991,869	1,547,695	464,164	489,104	505,5591
China Market place	371,993	615,062	215,917	316,760	301,074

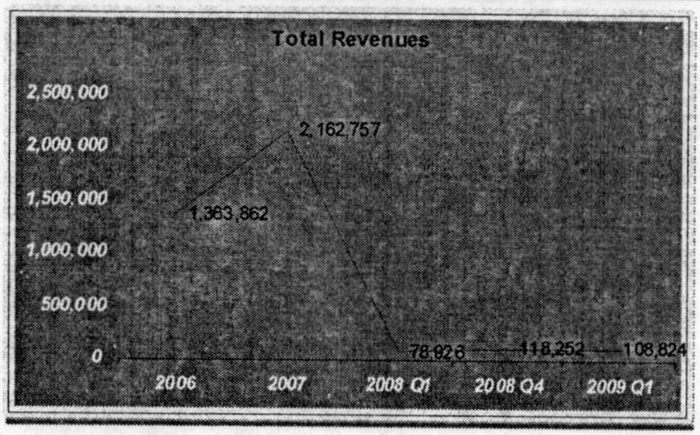

Key Highlights

- By 2012 it is expected that more than 1 trillion will be spent online by B2C Consumers.B2B spending will exceed this considerably.
- E-payment solutions are an important part of E-commerce transactions; however security issues continue to tarnish the industry.
- BuddeComm estimates revenue from mobile content and services (excluding SMS), accounts for around 7-

10% of total mobile revenues worldwide. SMS remains popular and accounts for a further 10% of total mobile data revenues.

- Online advertising growth is set to continue for the next few years, but will slow slightly in the wake of the US financial crisis. It is expected that online advertising will eventually account for around 20% of all advertising spend in some markets.
- Search services are central to almost everything that users do online, and this places leading search companies such as Google and Yahoo at an advantage. In the emerging Chinese market, Baidu and Alibaba also have a good foothold.
- Google is still the most popular website property worldwide; however individual countries and regions show unique differences with many local sites remaining popular. Other web properties proving popular across multiple markets include Yahoo, Microsoft and Wikipedia sites, Apple Inc, eBay and Amazon.

Summary

Preferences of online purchasing over stores

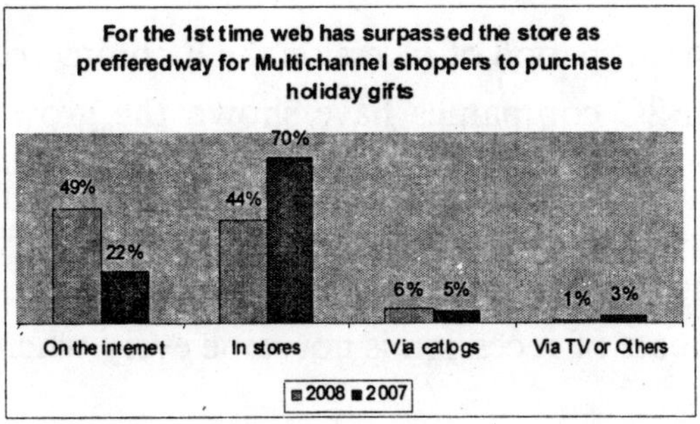

In 2008 the web has surpassed the stores for multichannel shoppers to purchase holiday gifts. In 2008 around 49% people purchased the products through web, while in 2007 this figure was 22% only. This shows that in recession has positive impact on E-commerce.

The future of E-commerce is going to depend upon a positive confluence of technology, regulation, laws. Culture, social issues, economics, vendors, competitors and all consumers. From the estimated future sales figures, that appears to be happening. Overall, E-commerce is and will be important for countries and firms that already possess the environment and the capabilities and capacity to utilize the Internet for sales purposes. While E-commerce may offer little initially to bring them to the industrial nation status, there will be dramatic increases in the well being of many third world countries. Economics, politics and competitive forces will also help bring them into the 21st Century of electronics, driven by the Internet that has no boundaries and is owned by no nation. A restructuring of worldwide channels of distribution will occur with concomitant new sales, sometimes to the detriment of existing industrialized nations, with a major contribution to the economic development of both industrialized and developing nations.

Even in this period of recession the E-commerce especially E-tailing, B2C companies have shown the growth towards positive side. When companies are cutting down their budgets, these companies are investing in E-Business during recession and reaping the profits because E-Business is a global business and the impact of recession is not same every where.

References

Books

- E-commerce-Business, technology, society 2008 by Kenneth C. Laudon and Carlo Guercio Traver

Websites

www.emarketer.com/Reports/All/Emarketer_2000577.aspx

www.seekingalpha.com

www.shipwire.com/help/c/recession_proof_ecommerce_business/

www.en.wikipedia.org/wiki/Alibaba_Group

www.investor.google.com/earnings.html

www.google.com/finance?q=GOOG

www.investor.google.com/releases.html

www.blogs.zdnet.com/BTL/?p=8033

www.mattdecuir.com/Google/financials.aspx

www.img.alibaba.com/ir/download/200905/E_1Q09_EarningsRelease.pdf

www.img.alibaba.com/ir/download/200803/Alibaba%20Earning%20Release_Eng.pdf

www.google.com

www.thehindubusinessline.com

www.harvardbusiness.org

www.protiviti.com/economiccrisis

http://www.wikinvest.com/stock/Amazon.com_(AMZN)?ref=topnav

http://jobsearchtech.about.com/od/companyprofiles/a/Amazon.htm

http://www.seattlepi.com/business/158315_amazon28.html

http://www.corporateinformation.com

http://www.crunchbase.com/company/amazon

http://www.chillibreeze.com/articles_various/Ecommerce.asp

http://wrightreports.ecnext.com/coms2
reportdesc_COMPANY_023135106

http://www.epaynews.com/item.php?news_id=6548

New Media and Democracy in Reterospective

INTRODUCTION

From the beginning of human civilization media exists. Its origin is as old as human being. In every era existing media has known as new media to the people of the society. Now we live in global village (Marshall McLuhan) where every moment some innovations and inventions in the field of science and technology is taking place and yesterday media is also adding innovation and making it better. May be it would be the demand of time but one thing should be cleared that. The traditional mode of media which was used by chosen few is now changed.

Now new media (internet) has broken the legacy of elite section of society. With the help of it any thing can be accessed by anyone. New knowledge which is known as power is democratized and new centers of power are emerged. In true sense, the benefit of this new media is not availed by the maximum population of India like countries, because of indirect controlled on these new media by the rulers. So somewhere access and democratic content are missing. All these issues will be detailed in my research paper whish is divided into three parts. In the first part the historical background of new media will be detailed, in the second part democratization of contents in new media will be discussed, And in the last chapter some suggestion will be given which can protect democracy contents and new media through which can strength and make a powerful society.

Objective: To protect the democracy with the use new media and to make a powerful society with the help of new media technology.

The Historical Background of New Media

With the Invention of Print machine around 3000 BC with the duplication of images. The use of round cylinder seals for rolling an impress onto clay tablets goes back to early Mesopotamian civilization before 3000 BC, where they are the most common works of art to survive, and feature complex and beautiful images. In both China and Egypt, the use of small stamps for seals preceded the use of larger blocks. In Europe and India, the printing of cloth certainly preceded the printing of paper or papyrus. This was probably the binging of print but it has played important role in social transformation of society maintain the democracy. According to the Indian Readership Survey large number of society read the news paper. Survey shows that the major population read the local language newspapers to be Dainik Jagran (with 16.429 million readers) and Dainik Bhaskar (with 14.448 million readers), both published in Hindi. Malayala Manorama newspaper which is published in Malayalam from, currently has a readership of over 9.9 million (with a circulation base of over 2 million copies) has the most circulation in other languages. Where as The Times of India is the most widely read English language newspaper (4.900 million), followed by Hindustan Times (3.9 million)

Italian born Guglielmo Marconi was fascinated by Hertz's discovery, and realised that if radio waves could be transmitted and detected over long distances, wireless telegraphy could be developed. He started experimenting in 1894 and set up rough aerials on opposite sides of the family garden. He managed to receive signals over a distance of 100 metres, and by the end of 1895 had extended the distance to over a mile. He approached the Italian Ministry of Posts and Telegraphs, informing them of his experiments.

Radio broadcast started in India with the setting up of a private radio service in Chennai, in the year 1924. In that same year, British government gave license to the Indian Broadcasting Company, to launch Radio stations in Mumbai and Kolkata. Later as the company became bankrupt, the government took possession of the transmitters and began its operations as the Indian State Broadcasting Corporation. In the year 1936, it was renamed All India Radio (AIR) and the Department of Communications managed it entirely. After independence, All India Radio was converted into a separate Department. All India Radio has five regional headquarters in New Delhi, for the North Zone; in Kolkata, for the East Zone; in Guwahati, for the North-East Zone, in Mumbai, for the West Zone; and in Chennai, for the South Zone.

In the year 1957, All India Radio was renamed Akashvani, which is controlled by the Ministry of Information and

Broadcasting. During the period of independence only a mere 6 radio stations existed through out the country. But during the late 1990s, the network of All India Radio extended to almost 146 AM stations. Moreover the Integrated North-East Service focused on reaching to the population in northeast India. All India Radio offers programmes in English, Hindi and numerous regional and local languages. In the year 1967, Commercial Radio services started in India. The initiative was taken by Vividh Bharati and Commercial Service, from the headquarters in Mumbai. Vividh Bharati accumulated revenues from widespread sponsorships and advertisements. During the mid-1990s, broadcasting was carried on from 31 AM and FM stations.

By 1994, there were around 85 FM stations and 73 short wave stations that linked the whole nation. The broadcasting technology in India is basically indigenous and reaches far and wide to various listeners like farmers who require various updated information on agriculture. Between 1970 and 1994, the amount of radio receivers increased manifold, almost five times. From the initial 14 million, the number increased to a staggering 65 million. The broadcast services from foreign countries are provided by the External Services Division of All India Radio. Almost 70 hours of news, entertainment programmes were broadcasted in 1994 in various languages with the help of 32 shortwave transmitters.

After Independence, Indian radio was regarded as a vital medium of networking and communication, mainly because of the lack of any other mediums. All the major national affairs and social events were transmitted through radio. Indian radio played a significant role in social integration of the entire nation. All India Radio mainly focused on development of a national consciousness as well as over all National integration. Programming was organised and created keeping in mind the solitary purpose of national political integration. This supported in prevailing over the imperative crisis of political instability, which was created after the Independence. Thus political enhancement and progressive nation building efforts were aided by the transmission of planned broadcasts.

All India Radio also provided assistance in enhancing the economic condition of the country. Indian radio was particularly designed and programmed to provide support to the procedure of social improvement, which was a vital pre-requisite of economic enhancement. The leading development beliefs of the time analysed the problems and hindrances in development as the primary ones in the developing nations.

Electronic television was first successfully demonstrated in San Francisco on Sept. 7, 1927. The system was designed by Philo Taylor Farnsworth, a 21-year-old inventor who had lived in a house without electricity until he was 14. While still in high school, Farnsworth had begun to conceive of a system that could capture moving images in a form that could be coded onto radio waves and then transformed back into a picture on a screen. Boris Rosing in Russia had conducted some crude experiments in transmitting images 16 years before Farnsworth's first success. Also, a mechanical television system, which scanned images using a rotating disk with holes arranged in a spiral pattern, had been demonstrated by John Logie Baird in England and Charles Francis Jenkins in the United States earlier in the 1920s. However, Farnsworth's invention, which scanned images with a beam of electrons, is the direct ancestor of modern television. The first image he transmitted on it was a simple line. Soon he aimed his primitive camera at a dollar sign because an investor had asked, "When are we going to see some dollars in this thing, Farnsworth?"

First television news covered the presidential nominating conventions of the two major parties, events then still at the heart of America politics, in 1952. The term "anchorman" was used, probably for the first time, to describe Walter Cronkite's central role in CBS's convention coverage that year. In succeeding decades these conventions would become so concerned with looking good on television that they would lose their spontaneity and eventually their news value. The power of television news increased with the arrival of the popular newscast, *The Huntley-Brinkley Report*, on NBC in 1956. The networks had begun producing their own news film. Increasingly, they began to compete with newspapers as the country's primary source of news.

During the last 50 years television, one of the greatest inventions of the scientific world has contributed immensely to the development of mankind. It has brought people of different countries and regions closer to each other, enabling them to learn about the culture and traditions flourishing in different parts of the world. It is perhaps the most powerful means of mass communication for education and entertainment.

The history of television in India started around later fifties. In 1955 a Cabinet decision was taken disallowing any foreign investments in print media which has since been followed religiously for nearly 45 years. Under this circumstances, television in India was introduced on September 15, 1959 in Delhi when UNESCO gave the Indian Government $20,000 and 180 philips TV sets. The programs were broadcast twice a week for an hour a day on such topics as community health, citizens' duties and rights, and traffic and road sense. In 1961 the broadcasts were expanded to include a school educational television project. The first major expansion of television in India began in 1972, when a second television station was opened in Bombay. This was followed by stations in Srinagar and Amritsar (1973), and Calcutta, Madras and Lucknow in 1975. In 1975, the government carried out the first test of the possibilities of satellite based television through the SITE ((Satellite Instructional Television Experiment)) program. For the first 17 years, broadcasting of television spread haltingly and transmission was mainly in black & white. By 1976, the government found itself running a television network of eight television stations covering a population of 45 million spread over 75,000 square kilometers. Faced with the difficulty of administering such an extensive television system television as part of All India Radio, the government constituted Doordarshan, the national television network, as a separate Department under the Ministry of Information and Broadcasting.

From its earliest beginnings on pages of paper and in brilliant minds, the Internet has always been an emerging technology and an emerging ideal. What follows is a selective and developing chronology of some of the most important events in the cultural and technological development of cyberspace and the internet.

1960s-1970s: ARPANET: Commonly thought of as the predecessor to the Internet and created by the US Department of Defenses Advanced Research Projects Agency (ARPA). The first known fully operational packet-switching network, the ARPANET was designed to facilitate communication between ARPA computer terminals during the early 1960s, at a time when computers where far too expensive for widespread usage. Though conception of the idea behind ARPANET began as early as 1962, the first stable link between multiple computers through the ARPANET occurred in 1969, ten years after the first conceptual network architectural models were initiated independently by Paul Baran and Donald Davies.

962-63: Working at the Massachusetts Institute of Technology (MIT), J.C.R. Licklider authored a series of memos concerning theoretical network structures. His concept of a Galactic Network envisioned a world-wide computer network in which computer terminals would be linked to one another, allowing anyone with access to a terminal the ability to access and send information to other computers and users. While working at the Department of Defenses Advanced Research Projects Agency (ARPA), Licklider stressed the importance of realizing this network design to his colleagues who would later go on to realize elements of the Galactic Network concept in the actualized form of the ARPANET, an early predecessor to the Internet.

1965: The first network experiment linking two computers takes place between the TX-2 computer by Lincoln Labs and the mainframe operated by the RAND corporations System Development Corporation. It is the first time in which two computers directly communicated with one another.

1970: The first radio network which makes use of random packet transmission, the Alohanet, is launched at the University of Hawaii.

1972: Robert Kahn exhibits the first public demonstration of the ARPANET at the International Computer Communication Conference. This public demonstration is also the first time that electronic mail (email) is exhibited and is a major catalyst for increasing interest in developing network technology. The first email programs called SNDMSG and READMAIL are written by Ray Tomlinson marking the beginning of one of the most widely used applications today.

1973: Robert Kahn, program manager for ARPAs Information Processing Techniques Office (IPTO), and Vinton Cerf (then a graduate student at Stanford University) worked together on the idea of developing internetworking or of connecting multiple networks in a more open form than the closed network of the ARPANET. Kahn and Cerf helped to develop a networking protocol that would allow an open-architecture for multiple networks to be joined together. This protocol later emerged as the Transmission Control Protocol/ Internet Protocol or TCP/IP. This new protocol would allow each individual network to stand alone such that if another network was brought down, it would not cause the collapse of all joined networks. Additionally, the new protocol conceptualized by Kahn and Cerf would involve no overall global manager and would join various networks together through what would later be known as routers and gateways. After the original TCP/IP protocol was written, what emerged as the Internet would result from ongoing experimentation and TCP/IP would emerge as on almost universal host protocol on which the Internet would be built. In the same year, the first international connections to the ARPANET are made with the addition of the University College of London and the Royal Radar Establishment in Norway.

1973-1975: While working at the Xerox Palo Alto Research Center, Robert Metcalfe develops a system which replaces radio transmission of network data with a cable that provides a larger amount of bandwidth, enabling the transfer of millions of bits of data per second in comparison with the thousands of bits per second when using a radio channel transmission. This system is originally known as the Alto Aloha network but which was later known as Ethernet. Metcalfe would later leave Xerox to found 3Com.

1974: Ted Nelson releases the countercultural technology manifesto Computer Lib in which Nelson advocates ordinary people learning about computer and network technology. Nelson also proposes hypertext as a way of organizing information, making it possible to link information in a less linear manner.

1975: The first commercially available popular personal computer, the Altair 8800 is introduced as a kit.

1976: Apple Computer founded by Steve Jobs and Steve Wozniak.

1977: ARPA funds the Bolt, Beranek, and Newman electronics company (intimately involved in the evolution of the ARPANET and the Internet) to use the TCP/IP protocol along with the emerging and popular Unix operating system. This is an example of the initial efforts of expanding the use of TCP/IP in the hopes of spreading a uniform standard protocol for internetworking which would allow for the emergence of the modern Internet.

1978: The first mass-marketed personal computer, the Apple II, is launched.

1979: Tom Truscott and Steve Bellovin make use of a UNIX program that allows files to be transferred between networked computers to exchange electronic newsletters between Duke University and the University of North Carolina by way of a dial-up connection. This system spreads and comes to be known as USENET. USENET distributes online forums or newsgroups concerning any number of topics across the Internet, allowing users to submit messages to news groups and communicate electronically in a informal manner.

1980-1982: At a meeting of computer scientists determined to expand accessibility to the ARPANET, Dave Farber reveals how a project which he and his colleagues at the University of Delaware are working on aims to build an inexpensive network by using dial-up phone links rather than radio or satellite as the means of connection. In 1982, after funding from the National Science Foundation, computer scientists build the PhoneNet system and establish Internet connections between the PhoneNet system, the ARPANET, and the first commercial network, Telenet. This CSNET system broadens overall access to the Internet and allows almost any school to access the network through less costly PhoneNet service. CSNET also greatly expands the geographic reach of the Internet by allowing e-mail between the United States, Germany, France, Japan, Korea, Finland, Sweden, Australia, Israel, and the United Kingdom. This incarnation of the Internet would continue to grow at an increasing rate by way of the increase in the number of networks that were attached to the Internet.

1981: 3Com announces an Ethernet product for workstation computers followed by a version for personal computers in 1982. The 3Com Ethernet networking system allows users to build more affordable local area networks (LANs) and has come to be the standard way of building personal networks. In the same year, IBM releases its own Personal Computer (PC) which will become the industry standard. Sun Microsystems launches the Sun I workstation.

1982-1983: ARPANET is split into two separate entities: MILNET to serve the needs of national defense and the military community and ARPANET which is primarily utilized by academics and researchers. This is the first step toward the commercialization of the Internet. The unofficial birth of the Internet occurs when both ARPANET and Defense Data Networks begin to use TCP/IP protocol. After an increase in the number of users and networks connected to the Internet, computer scientists begin to consider new methods of naming and addressing users and networks. The Domain Name System, first defined by Paul Mockapetris, Jon Postel, and Craig Partridge is created to divide Internet names between host names (x.com) and user names (user@x.com). This method of naming made the maintenance of host information more manageable. ARPA created six domains consisting initially of: edu (educational), gov (government), mil (military), com (commercial), org (other organizations), and net (network resources).

1990: ARPANET, thought outdated and obsolete is decommissioned. During the same year, Tim Berners-Lee,

Robert Cailliau, and other CERN scientists begin to create the first actual incarnation of the World Wide Web. Berners-Lee and his colleagues developed a shared format for hypertext documents which was named hypertext markup language or HTML. In addition to HTML, Berners-Lee and others created uniform resource locator (URL) as a standard address format that could specify the computer being targeted and the type of information being requested. URL and HTML significantly increased the possibility of interaction between users and networks across the Internet. URL also made different Internet services such as Usenet news accessible to all users employing the system.

1995: Bill Gates authors the now famous memo, The Coming Internet Tidal Wave. By 1995, the bulk of US internet traffic is routed through interconnected network service providers and Microsoft Windows 95 is launched. 1995 proves to be an eventful year in the formation of contemporary internet culture because it also sees the official launch of the online bookstore Amazon.com, the internet search engine Yahoo, online auction site Ebay, the Internet Explorer web browser by Microsoft, and the creation by Sun Microsystems of the Java programming language which allows for the programming of animation on websites giving rise to a new level of internet interactivity.

1996: The United States Congress passes the Communications Decency Act which is seen as a direct assault by censors on the ideals of free speech and information as promoted online. Congress passes the act in response to perceived public concern over the increased availability of pornography and other graphic and controversial matter made possible by the spread of the internet and cyberspace. The Communications Decency Act or Telecommunications Reform Act was an attempt by the US government to extend congressional oversight of laws aimed at regulated radio and television to the internet. John Perry Barlow responds with his now famous essay A Declaration of Independence for Cyberspace. Barlows essay is an impassioned declaration of cyberspace and the internet as realms of freedom and liberty that is not subject to the authority of national governments.

1999: The dawn of internet music and video piracy controversies rises with the introduction of the Napster file-sharing software by Shawn Fanning, a college student. During the same year, the Internet encounters the first malicious computer virus capable of automatically copying and sending itself to all email addresses listed in an infected users address book.

2000: After a bitter antitrust lawsuit, Microsoft is ordered to break into two separate businesses focusing on its highly successful Windows operating system and its other numerous software applications. 2000 would go down in Internet history as the rise and burst of the internet bubble. That year, the presence of internet consumer companies was widespread and visible in everyday life, including the visibility of .dotcom companies which paying millions of dollars for half-minute advertisements to air during the Super Bowl. When investors heard reports that Microsoft would be unable to settle its antitrust lawsuit with the government, the Dow Jones Industrial Average suffers the biggest one-day drop in its history up to that point. Microsoft will settle its lawsuit in 2001 allowing it to remain a single company, but in 2000, the internet revolution marches on with Google rise to become the worlds largest search engine and the first official instance of internet voting taking places in the United States during a Democratic Party primary in Arizona.

2002: Napster is shut down after it fails to win a lawsuit brought by the Recording Industry Association of America.

2003: The rise of spam; unsolicited junk mail messages begin to account for over half of all e-mail messages sent and received. Though the US Congress passes anti-spam legislation, the scourge of unsolicited email remains.

When someone said they thought TV was as old as newspapers the reply was, "Well, no. In the long history of mass media, newspapers are eight times older than television." That conversation highlighted the need for a clarification of the relative age of New Media. They are not that old, really. In fact, TV is about eight times older than many New Media.

W3C Web pages (Mosaic) – 1993

YAHOO! Yahoo! - January 1994

Wiki Wiki - March 1995

Blogging - December 1997

Google - September 1998

Wikipedia - January 2001

iPod - October 2001

Second Life - June 2003

MySpace - August 2003

Facebook - February 2004

Podcasting - September 2004

Digg - December 2004

YouTube - February 2005

Twitter - March 2006

Indian Internet History

Before the appearance of VSNL's GIAS, Internet had been in India for many years in the form of ERNET. However, it was not possible for many people to get access to it, as it was meant for only the educational and research communities. This followed the policy laid down by the American Internet manager NSF, at that time.

a. Educational Research Network (ERNET)

Internet in India was established almost 10 years ago, as ERNET. It was a joint undertaking of the Department of Electronics (DOE) of the Government of India, and the United Nations Development Program (UNDP), which provides technical assistance to developing nations. ERNET is one of the most successful operations that UNDP has funded. It established for India the idea that we can participate in the Internet. Currently ERNET operates many nodes and has a 64 Kbps link to USA via Mumbai.

All major nodes of ERNET are connected to each other using 9600 bps leased lines. These lines are being upgraded to 64 Kbps links. Over 200 academic and R&D groups exchange email with each other using ERNET. Over 8000 scientists and technologists have access to ERNET facilities. International access is provided over a 64 Kbps leased line, from NCST, Mumbai, to USA. Plans for ERNET include the creation of a satellite communication system to enable ERNET to reach locations which do not have good data communication links.

b. Gateway Internet Access Service (GIAS)

On August 15th 1995, Videsh Sanchar Nigam Limited (VSNL) — the Indian international trunk telephone carrier company — launched the Gateway Internet Access Service (GIAS). Subsequently, 6 nodes were established at Mumbai, Delhi, Madras, Calcutta, Bangalore and Pune. Each GIAS node is connected to Internet via high speed MCI circuits having a bandwidth of approximately 10 Mbps.

Users in remote areas of India can reach GIAS service via I-NET. The Department of Telecommunication (DOT) has a wide-spread network in India called I-NET, which has direct connectivity to each GIAS node.

The Negative Effect of New Media

1. Some bogus news given on the website may raise blood pressure and create negative feelings in the mind.
2. Over exposure to media may cause health problems also. The advertisements and many more shown in new media have got both positive and negative impact. The youths learn violence by seeing movies and many more sites. The over exposure to new media make them behave more aggressively, which spoils their future also.
3. The children get immense pleasure in playing video games and they spend hours together before computer, surfing through internet. They see both the good and the bad things through new media.
4. The youngsters wish to take part in these programs, which are unsuitable for many persons.
5. The Youth imitate their role models blindly. The negative things the celebrities do are often talked about. The controversies in the lives of the celebrities are often highlighted by the new media.

6. New Media often hypes the scintillating things about the celebrities. The negatives in society are highlighted with intent to awaken the people about the society of the modern days. But this hype is actually having a negative effect on society. Masses are seeing only the negatives around them. Controversies are constantly being bombarded on them. All this is responsible for influencing the society negatively.
7. People spending hours in front of a surfing the Internet have to suffer from eye problems and obesity. Long hours of new media exposure add to the sedentary nature of your lifestyle.
8. The negative psychological effects of media are seen in terms of new media changing the people's outlook of looking towards life. New Media being one of the prominent sources of looking at the outside world has changed the cultural and moral values of society. A majority of the youth believe in what is depicted by the new media. Many think all of it as true. Youngsters and children are bound to mix the reel and the real world and get highly influence by the mass media.

The Positive Effect of New Media

1. The distance is not at all a barrier now.
2. The new media helps common people to exchange information and it acts as a common platform.
3. The media helps to bring out the hidden talents of the people. The children learn many good things through new media.

4. The people learn many things, their reading habit increases and their vocabulary enhances by learning new words. Their knowledge increases by watching geographical channel, quiz programs and speeches by famous personalities of different fields.
5. The attitude, approach and behavior of the common people will also change, when exposed to new media.

6- The new media conducts polls and let public to take part in social issues. Through blogging in the internet and writing letters to the editor in newspapers, many people give voice about their opinion in different political and social matters.

Some suggestion for protect democracy contents and make a powerful society.

1. Legislation, including global harmonization
2. Operational law enforcement capacities through additional resources and powers
3. Make a global Policy for NEW Media (Law enforcement and judicial training)
4. Interagency International cooperation
5. Industry/law enforcement cooperation
6. International cooperation is required to check problems.

Women and Media-need for Paradigm Shift to Bring in Social Change

Introduction

Communication is extremely important for women's development and mass media play significant role. In all spheres of life, whether the controlling of population growth spread of literacy or improving the quality of life for vast masses, women have a crucial role to play. In this context, women have an important role to play to create awakening in them to achieve their potential as the prime movers of change in society. In today's world, print and electronic media play a vital role in effectively conveying message that needs to be conveyed. It is true that media have brought to light, as never before, certain misdemeanors against women but in a very subtle manner, it also perpetuated the stereotyped image of women as a householder and an inconsequential entity in the traditional value system. By gradually shaping public opinion, personal beliefs and even people's self perceptions, media influences the process of socialization and shapes ideology and thinking. Indian society is full of diversified cultures, traditions and beliefs. Our mass media's role as a social constructor and representative of women has greater responsibility in binding these complexities of culture and processes with the people of the society.

Key words: *Media, impact, stereotyping, gender sensitivity, empowerment.*

Introduction

Media is all pervasive and its functioning is very subtle. Media plays a vital role in dissemination of information. It is called the fourth pillar of democratic polity. The impact of media on our lives is a point which does not have to be labored, any longer. Radio, television, films and the printed word reach all of us in this age of information and each strives to perfect its modes of communications to become more effective as a medium. The roles of various media however, have stretched far beyond the supply of information now, because of the outreach and technological sophistication. In effect, this gives them the power to create reality. By gradually shaping public opinion, personal beliefs and even people's self perceptions, media influences the process of socialization and shapes ideology and thinking. The power of creating media reality is concentrated in the hands of a few people and their biases and their profit motives operate in the creation of a reality which is often distorted. Indian society is full of diversified cultures, traditions and beliefs. Our mass media's role as a social constructor and representative of people has greater responsibility in binding these complexities of culture and processes with the people of the society. In India, the status of women is undergoing a perceptible change. Women entering the labour market are on the rise, there is increase in the number of educated women, and heightened awareness of their mobilization to fight discrimination. The role of women in the family life has undergone significant changes. As an educated housewife or as a working woman, she has acquired a respectable place in society.

Accessibilty of Media to Women

The presence of women in media both in terms of numbers, whether absolute or in comparison with men and their status in terms of the position they occupy, is strongly influenced by the scene, not of their choice, but on account of the social and religious taboos which operated as legal sanctions, and even today operate as such, in many regions and communities, the constitution and laws not withstanding. Poverty, illiteracy, discrimination and male domination keep a vast majority of women away from the print media even as readers. As regards the electronic media, even where the community radio and television are available, either they are crowded out by the men, or on account of social inhibitions, women are unable to view or listen. Media has therefore largely come to be confined to the women in the middle and the higher classes, whether in the rural or urban areas and more particularly in the urban areas whether as passive consumers or as active players. The issue of women and the media can broadly be understood at two levels, both implicating and affecting each other:

- The participation of women in decision-making and expression in the media
- Representation or portrayal of women and gender relations in the media

Participation and Expression

At the most basic level, women are under-represented in media institutions. Those who are within the field are often not in decision-making positions. Although women are increasingly entering into media, top management is still largely male dominated and the culture of patriarchy is perpetuated through this disparity. There is a gender division of labor that is evident through the way that stories are assigned. 'Soft' issues like fashion, culture, arts and lifestyle are often consigned to women media practitioners, whereas 'hard' and what is considered 'serious' issues like finance, economics and politics are often within the purview of their male counterparts. The criteria of newsworthiness are similarly and consequently understood through this gendered lens. Headline materials often constitute of 'hard issues' whilst 'soft issues' are shunted to 'special' and supplementary segments of the media. Gender stereotyped views and attitudes, such as the attachment of productive incapacity and women's reproductive roles can hinder women's opportunities to assume decision-making positions. Further, sexual harassment has been particularly cited as one of the methods to control and exclude women from these positions. As media is becoming increasingly privatized and concentrated on a few transnational media giants, this can be a serious cause of concern when individuals within the field are left with little legal recourse to ensure the protection of their right to equal gender status. Government intervention often focuses on licensing and ownership as opposed to structures and practices within the institutions that discriminates against women, or prevents their views from being expressed. This contributes to the continued marginalization of women's themes in the media, their exclusion from socio-political institutions in the public sphere, and severely curtails media democratization in the promotion of diverse cultural, social and political worldviews.

Women's Portrayal in the Media

Throughout Asia, women have been portrayed in the media as victims, subservient, nurturing, sacrificing and objectified sexualized beings. This not only inaccurately represents the diversity of women's lives, roles and experiences within this complex and rich region, women's contributions to the socio-political and economic development of society are often neglected. The perpetuation of stereotypes in images and representation solidifies women's traditional roles and unequal gender relations in multiple ways. Most visibly, women are seen as mourners at tragedies or as victims of violence. The Global Media Monitoring Project found that out of the small number of women who were interviewees in news stories (14%), 29% of them were as victims of accidents, crimes or other events. This does not only represent women as helpless subjects without agency, it also fails to emphasize men's role as perpetrators in instances of violence against women. Further, the dissemination of these messages affects women's self-confidence, mobility and subsequently access and participation in public spaces for fear of assault. There are many more examples, such as women's portrayals in an increasingly consumer-driven culture and the commodification of women's bodies in advertising, pornography and conflict situations that can be cited and raised. These are two strategic objectives that have been outlined in the Beijing Platform for Action adopted by State governments at the Fourth World Conference for Women in 1995. They address broadly the two levels of discrimination which are to increase the participation and access of women to expression and decision-making in and through the media and new technologies of communication and promote a balanced and non-stereotyped portrayal of women in the media.

The various types of media are:

1. Electronic (Radio, Television etc.)
2. Print

Electronic Media

Radio and Television combined with satellite channels provide wide coverage on almost important aspects of life. Doordarshan & All India Radio have captured good audience size not only in cities but also even in semi-urban and rural areas. The program contents of both All India Radio (AIR) and Doordarshan give priority mainly to entertainment- based programmes. Women issues and their development programmes are reflected poorly in both the media. Lack of adequate planning and importance to women's programmes loses the target audience group. The Indian television programmes on women are generally based on the lives and cultures of urban society. In quantity there have been very few, in quality very poor programmes are concerned with the problems of women in rural areas. The main reason behind this is the commercial nature of Doordarshan, commercial sponsors and advertisers do not prefer women issue programmes, which they think are not very popular and or are liked by few audience. Television has been called the most real form of media. It is the real representation of women in TV and it affects the mindset of those who watch the television, specially the negative and debasing image of women as represented through money-spinning advertisements and serials. The systematic oppression of women by men is being projected by television. Many argue against the current trend of female TV characters opting to give up their career. Sex stereotype is also very much evident in television portrayal of men and women in their appointed roles. Various Tv. channels show women characters dominating the serials and are either shown as silently suffering characters or as vindictive, revenge seeking, glamorous vamps.

Print Media

The print media which include newspapers, periodicals, newsletters and other channels are relied upon by the people as credible source of information, education and entertainment. The print media are known for fearless criticism and service. The media reflects events taking place in society and provides a platform for dialogue and debate on issues which can generate social changes. While electronic media carries more immediate weight on focusing attention on various issues, it is print media which has more persistent and lasting effect. It is felt that the way women are being projected in the print and electronic media is a reflection on the whole society. Though there is no authentic research done in this area it is estimated by those working in this field that print media, both daily and weekly, that only about 7 to 10 % of the total coverage is on women's issues and about half of these are related to sex, prostitution, glamour, entertainment and crime. In the past few years, there has been an improved and increased reportage of issues related to women in the media particularly in the print. News related to women though still marginal have started to occasionally occupy important slots like the editorial, feature news, front-page news etc. However, women's visibility in the news is still dominated by sensational stories of glamour, sex, domestic violence and other forms of violence. Stories like women coping with adversity or building their lives are largely missing. Issues affecting women, their vast experiences and their lives, barely find their way into the mainstream media. Likewise, very few informative pieces or feature columns are published for women informing them about their legal rights, or about their potential for political activity. Many other studies have also established that when women appear in the news, they are mostly projected as passive victims or passive reactors to public events in news media. They hardly appear as speakers or participants in public event.

Newspapers

The lack of gender sensitivity in the media is evidenced in the failure to eliminate gender-based stereotyping. Generally, the media do not provide a balanced portrayal of women's diverse lives and their contributions to society in a changing world, often reinforcing stereotyped images of women and their roles in society. It is a common practice additionally to assess the professional success of a woman through questions and claims about her related to being a good mother and a wife. This is exactly the type of writing in the media that undermines the efforts of activists, who aim to establish gender equality in all areas of society. The prevailing portrayal of women in mainstream daily newspapers has the following characteristics:

- Positive images of women have a narrow scope and are based on new stereotypes of women's success like a pop star, a beauty queen, and a sport's woman with an outstanding result.

- There is an absence of the image of an active, assertive workingwoman, of a successful businesswoman, or a positive image of a woman politician.
- Average women are nearly always portrayed as victims of poverty, social injustice, domestic violence and organized crime.
- Misogyny in the form of rude jokes, mockery or open verbal aggression have become an accepted way of a systematic backlash against women activists working for women's political empowerment consisting of issues like freedom of abortion, freedom of sexual orientation, human rights.

It is the culture pages that help to round out the portrayal through the reviews of exhibitions by women artists, performances by female musicians, critiques of plays produced or acted by women, but here too are the seductive Swapnasundaris and Mallika Shehrawats or the sexy silk Smithas and the razzle dazzle Kareena who the camera and the pen focus on. Only the Sports pages carry some positive news of the achievements of women athletes and players like Sania Mirza. Yet even here, when women achieve positive or even spectacular results, men find ways of undermining or ridiculing their success. The presence of women in media both in terms of numbers, whether absolute or in comparison with men, and their status in terms of the position they occupy is strongly influenced by the scene, not of their choice, but on account of the social and religious taboos which operated as legal sanctions, and even today operate as such, in many regions and communities. Even in those regions and communities where the social and religious taboos can no longer be enforced, poverty, illiteracy, discrimination and male domination keep a vast majority of women away from the print media even as readers. The positive side of women's progress and their contribution for national development has not been adequately discussed in the print media. The emphasis on stories about women, about their struggle for recognition is only the surface trimming. The actual message to audience still is that society opposes the liberation of women.

Magazines and Journals

Magazines differ markedly from newspapers in content, time element and methods of operation. In contrast to daily newspapers with its hurry-up headlines, magazines are published weekly, fortnightly, monthly or sometimes quarterly, because these publications usually deal with subjects in greater depth than newspapers do. Magazines fulfill four major purposes in our lives. They inform, guide and entertain the average reader. They also assist commerce through advertising. Information is imparted chiefly by printing news, while in depth articles and features help to give the reader the background necessary to understand intelligently current events and ideas. Entertainment is provided through numerous articles, jokes and cartoon strips. A newspaper is designed for family reading while magazines in most instances aim carefully at special interest audience. Indian Magazines contain primarily and predominantly volumes of advertisements and sexist writings. A vast majority of Indian Magazines are known for the portrayal of women as sex objects, consumers and slaves. Women journals are mostly elitist and sexist. They are not in a position to advocate the course of women and rejuvenate our socio-political economic and cultural orders. The targeted readerships of these magazines are the upper and lower middle classes living in cities. Most of women's journals consistently seek to direct women's energies into a narrow channel to define their concerns, pre-occupations and aspirations with an arbitrarily imposed feminine framework. The impression created is that the outside world belongs to men and the issues which arise there do not affect women except indirectly through the men related to them. Women's magazines confer status on women as a group and make womanly things a serious business. They provide a public platform and a symbolic social order which consistently offers a woman cheap and accessible source of positive evaluation alongside practical directions for fulfilling her potential as a consumer. They also preach the ideal of a woman's power of self determination by their overwhelming emphasis on self- help.

Indecent posters and boardings displayed everywhere are the crude reminders of distorted images and attitudes to women. Popular magazines with large circulations flash vulgar and obscene glossy photographs on their cover pages. The advertising world continues to use women to peddle its products and to present women as sexual objects. The image of the educated woman is typecast as insensitive, self-centered and uncaring. The economically independent woman is shown as domineering and ruthless. The woman is considered ideal only when she is in her nurturing roles and as a supportive supplement to man. The coverage of women issues in the English print media and in the Indian language press differs in a number of ways. This is quite expected due to the very difference of readership profiles and other characteristics. The regional language press has its compulsions to be biased, inflammatory, sensational, communal and partisan. This is so as it serves only a small segment of readers who are conservative and traditional and read such papers only to replenish and refresh their established beliefs.

There have been several studies of print media with regard to women which have found the print media guilty of sexism, distortion of image of women and propagation of sex stereotypes like mothers, housewives, dependant, passive, etc. The other side of such misinterpretation is that in most popular print media women are seldom shown as working women who are capable professionals, labourers, farmers. Rather the predominant image is that of the self-sacrificing housewife. The analysis done of the so- educational media like children's books, adult literacy primers for women shows that they are sexist and they perpetuate sex-stereotypes. The Print Media has also seen a growth spurt in the recent years particularly with regard to women and development magazines. The journals are mostly qualified for modern society and could be said to be positively harmful to the development of women as conscious individuals aware of themselves and aware of the society around them. If a woman wins a beauty contest, magazines or newspapers in particular give much importance to the news and even take her photographs on cover page but, at the same time if a woman gets the Nobel Prize she gets limited coverage. Here the difference of judgment in women's issues is quite marked in our media.

Information in the print reinforces the stereotype and traditional roles of women in society. In order to enhance the status and position of women in society the information messages should portray women in career oriented, lead roles and in a holistic image, which is truly representative of Indian culture and ethos. Media is an issue is related to all women's issues and it affects not only urban women but all women and all men. By reinforcing sex stereotypes and constantly glorifying motherhood and sub-servient wifehood the print media makes it difficult for women to break out of these prescribed roles, norms and behaviour patterns. Such conservative depictions reduce the few statements about sex equality and equal participation of women contained in the Constitution to mere window dressing. This is not a plea of literary writing for women to be scoured but to redress the enormous harm done by existing portrayals and images in print media. Women must resist being sold in this manner and it is time they took the power of this medium in their own hands to create truth in their idiom or the pressures of the mass market will make their struggle for change increasingly difficult. The status of women has not improved noticeably despite the government's and the media's claim about social justice towards women. What is needed is a wider change in the social outlook.

Clearly, the media does not provide a balanced picture of women's diverse lives and contributions to society in a changing world. Much remains to be done with regard to the participation, portrayal and access of women to the media and its impact on and use as an instrument for the advancement and empowerment of women. What our country needs in the present context are minimum regulation and more enablement. Media reinforces the conservative view of women and ignores their economic participation and contribution, especially that of rural women, over 50% of whom are directly involved in economic activities, in addition to housework and childcare. All this means that media, instead of challenging the view that women are inferior, subservient, unimportant, reinforces it and it establishes man as the active force, the doer, the one who matters. The needs and concerns, the problems they face are not articulated publicly, no public thinking and debates are initiated on their real concerns. Because their concerns and interests remain unarticulated in the print, women also remain neglected.

Conclusion

As media practitioners and institutions, independent code of ethics that specifically addresses gender issues within this field can be developed and implemented. These codes can be further modified to ensure that sexist and stereotyped coverage of women are considered ethically unacceptable within the industry. Self-regulatory mechanisms such as adoption of sexual harassment policies within media institutions can dismantle one of the real obstacles that hinder women's full participation in media. Consistent and sustained capacity building of all members within media institutions whether male or female, reporters, editors or producers on gender issues can not only raise awareness on the complexities and implications of gender dynamics and power relations within this field, but also broaden the base of experts that are able to work with these issues meaningfully. More airtime can be allocated to issues related to women that break away from the usual areas traditionally considered as women's issues. One concrete example would be to increase the portrayal of women as significant contributors to society as leaders, workers and thinkers, not just as carers, sex objects or victims. The development of appropriate alternative and community media can also enable the dissemination of diverse expressions and experiences, particularly from marginalized groups who are better able to own and manage them at the community level. Media has immense power in this process. It is one of the primary institutions which help shape the world. Taking accountability in this role and interrogating its own practices, perceptions, expectations and visions is crucial to imagine a society that is abundant in diversity, critical of inequality and resistant to marginalisation.

The issue of gender should be at the forefront of discussions concerning freedom of expression. International commitments such as the WSIS Declaration of Principles and a Plan of Action and the Beijing Platform for Action need to be aligned to understand women's rights and gender equality as a cross cutting principle. Particularly in light of the development of digital information and communication technologies in media that have the capacity to transcend national boundaries and enable proliferation of discourses at unprecedented breadth and speed, gender dimensions crucially need be to be surfaced and addressed. Otherwise, the move towards building Information Societies for economic, social and political development will be one that is substantively impoverished for want of principles in equality and non-discrimination. On the other hand, media can be utilized for projecting the true and positive image of women and to wipe out her traditional passive image that has been imprinted on the mind of the society as a whole, including the women. The potentiality of media as a powerful instrument of social change has first to be used to restore 50% of the humanity to its proper pedestal. Change has to be brought about not only in the status of women but in the attitude of the society towards them. Priority has therefore necessarily to be given to changing image of women, from a passive onlooker and recipient, to that of a positive doer and achiever.

However the scenario is not so depressing with the advent of women reporters and the presence of some senior women journalists in positions of responsibility. That has made a significant difference to the coverage of women's issues in the press. They have observed that in the past ten years, women's issues have increasingly, though sporadically begun to make news and to be considered worthy of comment. This is due to the growth of the contemporary, women's movement in India, with women's groups becoming steadily more active and vocal. The English press and the other language papers in India have been doing well as far as the coverage of women is concerned. Lead reports, articles, editorials, features and news analysis have been published on women's issues. For media to promote balanced and non-stereotype portrayal of women in their multiple roles, it is imperative that government, media, NGOs and private sector should come together and forge joint strategies to promote gender equality and gender justice. In its new-found expansive role, media should foster a broad ethical content and moralizing impulse in the society so essential for the emergence of a civil society. Moreover for the society's abiding benefit media must nurture and transmit humane values of civilization. They must take upon themselves the proactive role of a protector and a promoter of human rights, gender justice and democratic order.

References

1. Agrawal, Bina, Bhasin, Kamla. Women and Media, Ch-1, pp 14-30. Vikas Publications, New Delhi.
2. Abraham, N. (1988). Women's Liberation and Indian Media, Vol-25, No. 6, pp. 22-25. Vidura, New Delhi.
3. Allen, D., Rush, R.R., Kaufman, S.J. (1996). Women transforming communications- Global Intersections. Sage Publications, New Delhi.
4. Agrawal, Vinod, C. and Rai, Kumkum (1988). Women Television and Rural Development. pp. 56-64. National Publishing House.
5. Afsar Bano. (2003).Indian Women-The changing face, Kalaso Books, Delhi.
6. Bathla, Sonia (1998). Women, Democracy and the media - cultural and political Representations in the Indian Press. pp 77-113. Sage Publications, New Delhi.
7. Batra, P. & Grover, I. (1994) Magazine Circulation and Reading Habits of Rural Women', Media and Development, Har Anand Publication.
8. Chopra, Anshu (2008). **Portrayal of Women in Print Media.** Dissertation submitted to Women & Study Development Centre, Delhi University.
8. De, Utpal Kumar, Ghosh, Bholanath (2004). Issues on empowerment of women, Monit Publications, New Delhi.
9. Jain, Devaki and Rajput, Ram (Ed.) (2003). Narratives from the Women's studies Family. Sage Publications, New Delhi.
10. Menon, Latika (1997). Gender Issues and Social Dynamics. Kanishka Publishers, New Delhi.
11. Mahapatra, Subhasini (2006).Status of women towards empowerment. Rajat Publications, New Delhi.

12. Nirmal J & Vardarajan Dhulasi B. (2005). Empowerment of women. Serials Publications, New Delhi.
13. Prasad Kiran (Ed.) (2005). Women and Media - Challenging Feminist Discourse. The Women's Press, Priyadarshini Vihar, New Delhi.
14. Reddy, P.A, Jayalakshmi, M. (2004). Exposure of women to mass media. pp.50-56. Classical Publishing Company, New Delhi

Index